The Meon Valley Railway

April 1983

ISBN 0 946184 04 6

Published by
Kingfisher Railway Productions
PO Box 8, Southampton, SO9 7AJ

Printed by
Biddles Limited, Martyr Road, Guildford, Surrey.
Typesetting by
Inset, 356 Portswood Road, Southampton, Hampshire.

Contents

Acknowledgements

I wish to thank the following people and organisations for their help in the preparation of this book; British Railways Board, John Fairman, Reg Gould, Deborah Greenep, Edward Griffith, Maurice Gunner, Hampshire Chronicle, Hampshire Museums Service, Public Records Office, Kew, Kevin Robertson and the Winchester Library.

Preface

The Meon Valley Railway will always remain in my mind as one of my favourite photographic haunts. Opened in 1903, as part of a through route from London via Alton to Portsmouth, and laid out to main line standards, it never fulfilled its original purpose, and remained a backwater to the end of its days.

Who better to chronicle its story than Ray Stone, a life long resident of West Meon, whose grandfather was parcels agent there for 40 years, who observed its rise and fall at close quarters, and had the sad task of assisting at the demolition.

I call to mind two unconventional trips, once in 1948 on the footplate of the engine hauling the up afternoon goods train from West Meon to Alton, an interesting experience and in the mid '70's, the motive power being an old Austin Mini fitted with flanged wheels by Charles Ashby, who at that time had a lease of the remnant of the line from Droxford to Mislingford.

As an old Guildford driver once said to me, "what a beautiful line that was that ran through the Meon Valley, such wonderful scenery, that I always thought I was in a world of fantasy".

E.C. Griffith

Obviously delighted with their new railway, a resident of West Meon sent this locally produced light hearted card to a friend in 1911. Author's collection.

Early schemes

The Meon Valley Railway, as it finally appeared on the scene in June 1903, was the outcome of a number of schemes to provide through routes from London to the south coast through such places as Aldershot, Windsor and Ascot. Earlier projects had plans to use land to the south of West Meon, such as the Alton and Petersfield railway, which as early as 1851 wanted to use the southern part from West Meon to Fareham, and the L.S.W.R. who had obtained an act in 1864 for a branch from Ropley to Meonstoke which would probably have provided a station at Warnford before joining the proposed Bishops Waltham to Petersfield line.

Later still in 1881, the Windsor, Aldershot and Portsmouth Railway had plans in mind for a junction at Farnham with a line hence through Tilford, Frensham and Selborne, to East Tisted, on through to West Meon where it would veer east to Hambledon and on to Cosham. This proposed line would have necessitated gradients of the magnitude of 1 in 80 and three or more tunnels of some great length.

Looking back in time, one wonders what it was that really prompted the promoters to invest vast sums of money to build railway lines over land which was in those days mostly agricultural and thinly populated. It would seem that the stations and railway facilities were provided more for the large houses and the estates of the landed gentry than for the local villages en route as the Station itself was sometimes a mile from the village.

Eventually on 3rd June 1897 the LSWR obtained The South Western (Meon Valley) Railway Act and the chosen route appeared as the "Meon Valley Railway" from Alton to Fareham, to be part of a through route from Waterloo to Gosport and Stokes Bay and also to provide a secondary route to Portsmouth.

The line, without doubt,was to provide a most picturesque route, but although it was picture postcard in appearance it turned out to be a very difficult and expensive task for the contractors whose job it was to construct this 22½ mile railway.

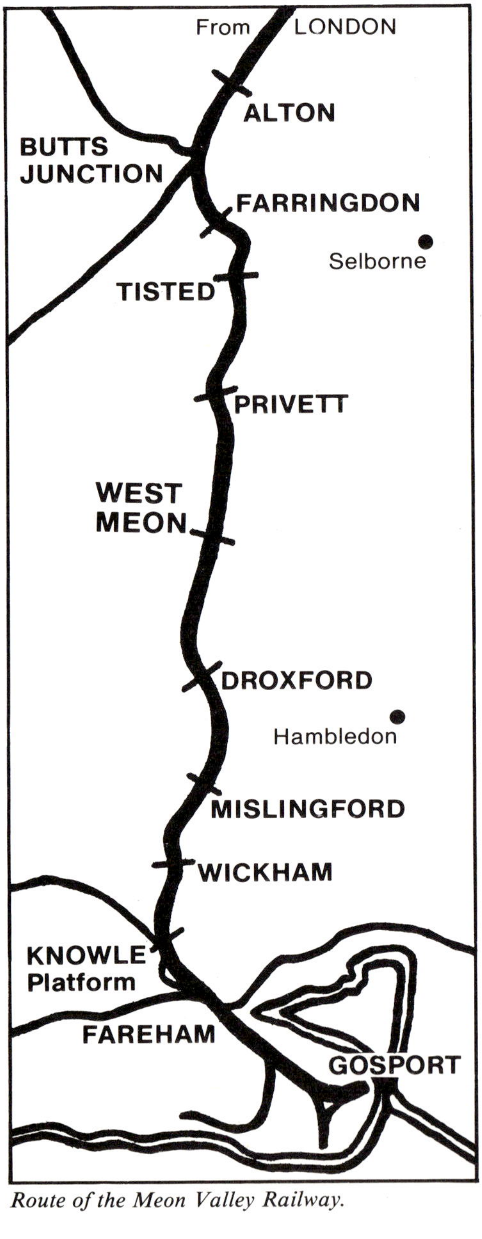

Route of the Meon Valley Railway.

CONSTRUCTION PHOTOGRAPHS

The rare selection of photographs of the Construction period have been kindly supplied by Mr. D.H. Foster-Smith. They are believed to have been taken by his grandfather, David Smith, who travelled around with the Navvy Mission looking after the social needs of the navvies and their families.

LOCOMOTIVES USED DURING THE CONSTRUCTION

The locomotives listed below, eight in total, were used at various points along the route during the construction years. The first five were delivered new from their makers to the site, the remaining three having worked elsewhere in the country on other projects. Two further 0-4-0STs, named *Blanche* and *Annie,* are believed to have been involved also.

Number/Name	Wheel	Cylinders	Builder	Builders Number	Date Built
8	0-6-0ST	IC	MW	1400	1899
10	0-4-0ST	OC	MW	1419	1899
11	0-4-0ST	OC	MW	1420	1899
13	0-6-0ST	IC	MW	1488	1900
EVELYN	0-6-0ST	IC	HC	542	1900
JUBILEE	0-4-0ST	OC	MW	991	1887
CORRIB	0-6-0ST	IC	MW	1220	1891
	0-4-0ST	OC	MW	1343	1897

Construction

It was planned from the beginning that this particular line was to be made wide enough for a second track to be laid if it ever became necessary, and enough land was acquired with this purpose in mind, and all bridges and tunnels were built wide enough for two lines.

It is interesting to note from the LSWR "Terrier" of the Meon Valley Railway, (Solicitors Office Copy) the purchases of land from local landowners. The sum of 5/- (25 pence) was paid to a Mrs. E. Major in the Parish of Fareham on 15th October 1898, as a receipt for compensation in respect of tenants interest in a cottage. In great contrast, in the Parish of Wickham on 17th July 1899, J.C. Garnier Esq. and others were paid £7,500 for over 23 acres of land. In total the land sales amounted to 298 acres.

After several conferences with the principal landowners, the L.S.W.R. recommended to their shareholders that this line should not be constructed as a light railway with sharp curves and steep gradients, so as to reduce expense, but as a first class railway with curves and gradients suitable for the passage of trains at express speed.

The contracts for construction were entrusted to Messrs. Relfe and Son of Plymouth who took some six years to complete from start to finish, and the engineer in charge was Mr. W. R. Galbraith, the Consulting Engineer of the London and South Western Railway. The Resident Engineer was Mr. Henry Byers and the architectural work of the stations was carried out by Mr. T. Phillips Figgis of London.

The contractors supplied detailed estimates for building the line in December 1896. These were to include costs for what they term as Railway No. 1 and Railway No. 2, and the

0-6-0ST "Corrib", one of the locomotives used during construction.

widening of the line from Alton to Butts Junction. Railway No. 1 was a section of just over 2 miles from Fareham to Knowle, using a route to the south of the Bishopstoke to Gosport Railway. It was planned to avoid the Fareham Tunnels, which since 1841 had caused considerable problems. This section was not constructed in the beginning, although the first few yards were utilised for storage of ballast wagons during construction of Railway No. 2, which was from Knowle to Butts Junction. The detailed estimates are on the accompanying pages.

In 1898 work commenced at various points between the Butts and Farringdon, with long shallow cuttings being dug at Chawton, the chalk from which formed the long embankment to cross the Alton to Winchester road. It was not until 1902 that the cutting from Alton Station to the Butts Junction was widened to make room for the new line. At around this time, the station at Alton was altered to accommodate Meon Valley trains. The down platform was made into an island, thus allowing Meon Valley bound journeys independent access.

The soil formation was formed almost entirely of the easily workable chalk, but was almost completely devoid of water which was necessary for the contractors engines and also for concreting, so that deep artesian wells had to be sunk at great expense.

The section from Alton to Butts Junction, was widened especially for accommodating Meon Valley trains. Here we see the contractors building the actual Meon Valley line, which branched off towards Farringdon.

Work in progress at Butts Junction.

ESTIMATE OF EXPENSE of the Works proposed to be authorised by the London and South Western Railway (Meon Valley Railway) Bill.

Railway No. 1					Whether Single or Double.
		Miles.	F.	Chs.	
Length of Line . . .		2	0	6·75	Single, with land and over-bridges for double line.

Earthworks:—	Cubic Yards.	Price per Yard. s. d.	£ s. d.	£	s.	d.
Cuttings—Rock	—	—	—			
Soft Soil . .	285,500	1 2	16,654 3 4			
Roads . . .	—	—	—			
Total	285,500	—	16,654 3 4	16,654	3	4
Embankments, including Roads . 158,000 Cubic Yards						
Bridges—Public Roads . . . . . Number 2				1,200	0	0
Accommodation Bridges and Works				2,000	0	0
Tunnels . . . . None						
Viaducts . . . . None						
Culverts and Drains				500	0	0
Metallings and Fencings of Roads and Level Crossings . .				200	0	0
Gatekeepers' Houses at Level Crossings . . None						
Permanent Way, including Fencing:—						
Miles. 2, F. 0, Chs. 6·75 at	Cost per Mile. £ 2,800 s. 0 d. 0			5,836	5	0
Permanent Way for Sidings, and Cost of Junctions . .				1,000	0	0
Stations . . . . None						
				27,390	8	4
Contingencies, 10 per cent.				2,739	0	10
				30,129	9	2
Land and Buildings:— A. 25, R. 0, P. 0				5,200	0	0
Total . . . . . £				35,329	9	2

Wm. R. GALBRAITH, } *Engineers.*
E. ANDREWS, }

Railway No. 2.				Whether Single or Double.
	Miles.	F.	Chs.	
Length of Line . .	22	2	6·35	Single, with land and over-bridges for double line.

Earthworks:—	Cubic Yards.	Price per Yard. s.	d.	£	s.	d.	£	s.	d.
Cuttings—Rock	—	—		—					
Chalk & Soft Soil	1,195,000	1	1	64,729	3	4			
Roads	18,120	1	2	1,057	0	0			
Total . . .	1,213,120	—		65,786	3	4	65,786	3	4

		£	s.	d.
Embankments, including Roads .	1,261,500 Cubic Yards			
Bridges—Public Roads	Number 33	24,850	0	0
Accommodation Bridges and Works		25,000	0	0
Tunnels		39,900	0	0
Viaducts		10,000	0	0
Culverts and Drains and River Bridges.		7,500	0	0
Metallings and Fencings of Roads and Level Crossings .		3,500	0	0
Gatekeepers' Houses at Level Crossings . .	None			
Permanent Way, including Fencing:—				
Miles. 22, F. 2, Chs. 6·35 at	Cost per Mile. £ 2,800 s. 0 d. 0	62,522	5	0
Permanent Way for Sidings, and Cost of Junctions . .		10,000	0	0
Stations		20,000	0	0
		269,058	8	4
Contingencies, 10 per cent.		26,905	16	10
		295,964	5	2
Land and Buildings:— A. 270 R. 0 P. 0		52,250	0	0
Total . . . . . £		348,214	5	2

Wm. R. GALBRAITH,
E. ANDREWS, } *Engineers.*

Widening of Farnham, Alton and Winchester Line.	Miles.	F.	Chs.	Whether Single or Double.
Length of Widening .	1	3	4·50	Single.

Earthworks—	Cubic Yards.	Price per Yard. s.	d.	£	s.	d.	£	s.	d.
Cuttings—Rock	—	—		—					
Soft Soil . . .	35,700	1	1	1,933	15	0			
Side Cutting . .	20,000	1	2	1,166	13	4			
Roads	—	—		—					
Total	55,700	—		3,100	8	4	3,100	8	4

		£	s.	d.
Embankments, including Roads . .	55,700 Cubic Yards			
Bridges—Public Roads	Number 3	1,500	0	0
Accommodation Bridges and Works		500	0	0
Tunnels	None			
Viaducts	None			
Culverts and Drains		100	0	0
Metallings and Fencings of Roads and Level Crossings.	None			
Gatekeepers' Houses at Level Crossings . . .	None			
Permanent Way, including Fencing :—				
Miles 1, F. 3, Chs. 4·50 at	Cost per Mile £2,500 0s. 0d.	3,578	2	6
Permanent Way for Sidings, and Cost of Junctions . .		1,000	0	0
Stations		4,000	0	0
		13,778	10	10
Contingencies, 10 per cent.		1,377	17	1
		15,156	7	11
Land and Buildings:— A. 3 R. 0 P. 0		800	0	0
Total . . . £		15,956	7	11

Wm. R. GALBRAITH, } *Engineers.*
E. ANDREWS, }

GENERAL SUMMARY OF TOTAL COST.

Total cost of Railway No. 1	£ 35,329	9	2
Total cost of Railway No. 2	£ 348,214	5	2
Total cost of Widening of Farnham, Alton and Winchester Line	£ 15,956	7	11
Grand Total . . .	£ 399,500	2	3

WM. R. GALBRAITH, } *Engineers.*
E. ANDREWS, }

In accordance with the foregoing details, WE ESTIMATE the whole expense of the undertaking under the London and South Western Railway (Meon Valley Railway) Bill (so far as it is a Bill of the second class specified in the Standing Orders) at THREE HUNDRED AND NINETY-NINE THOUSAND FIVE HUNDRED POUNDS TWO SHILLINGS AND THREE PENCE.

Dated this 29th day of December, 1896.

WM. R. GALBRAITH, } *Engineers.*
E. ANDREWS, }

Say £400,000.

This is a map from the "Terrier" of 1897 showing the land purchased for Railway No. 1 at Fareham. The route was to be between the Bishopstoke to Gosport Railway (now known as the Eastleigh to Fareham line) and the Netley to Fareham Railway (now the Southampton to Portsmouth line).

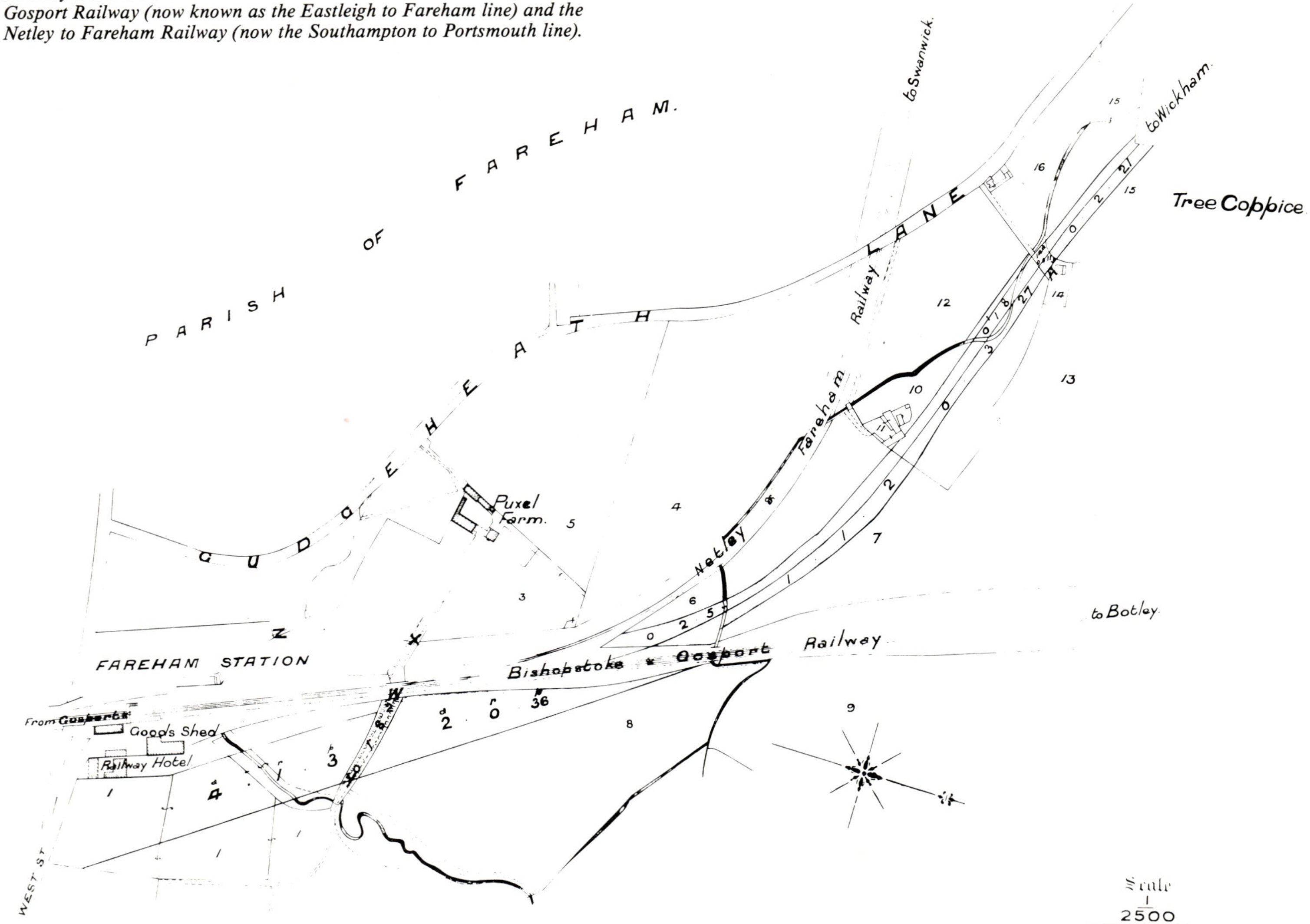

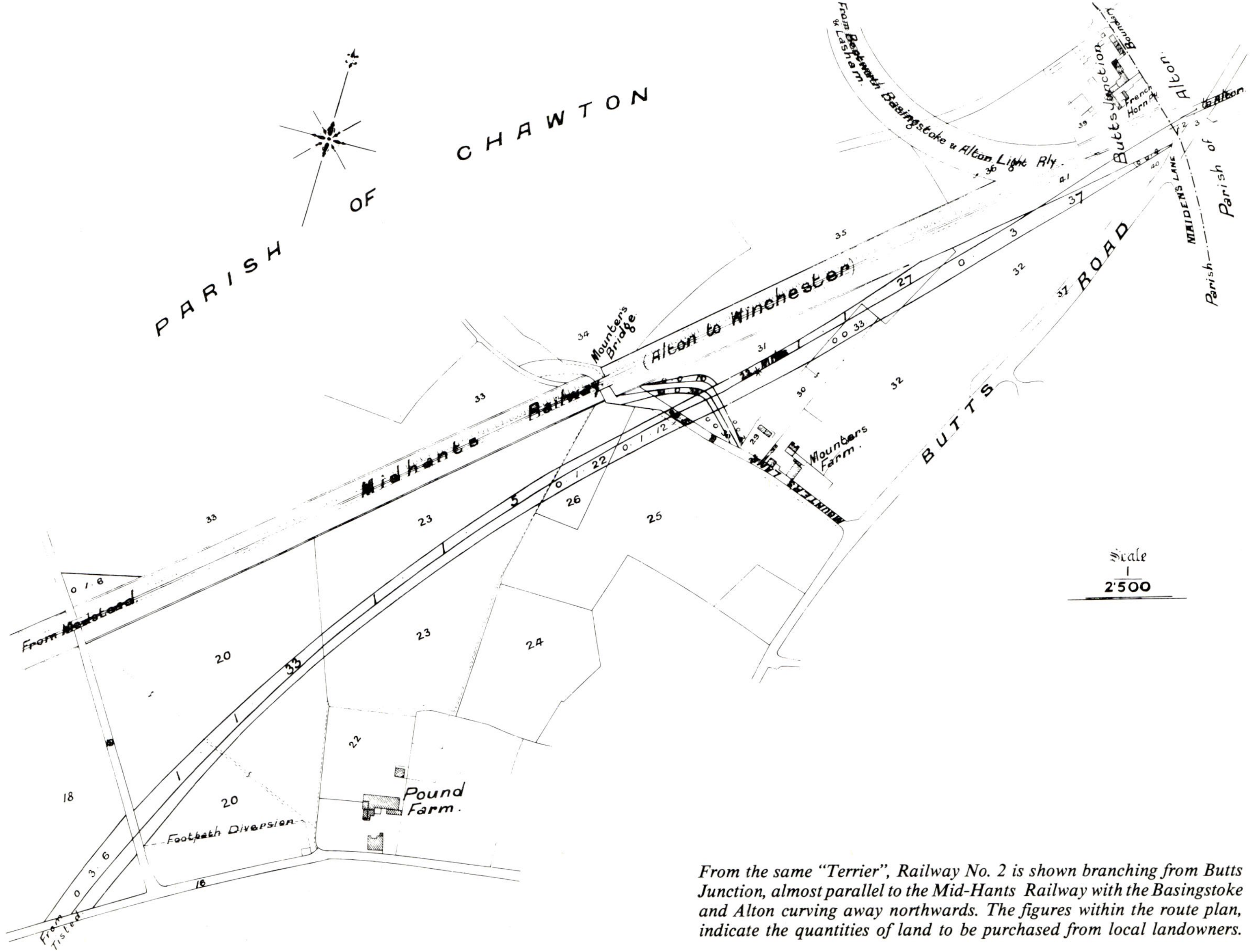

From the same "Terrier", Railway No. 2 is shown branching from Butts Junction, almost parallel to the Mid-Hants Railway with the Basingstoke and Alton curving away northwards. The figures within the route plan, indicate the quantities of land to be purchased from local landowners.

FARRINGDON

Originally spelt Faringdon – a small siding was built here for the transporting of farm produce. In later days, a Halt for passenger use was built as an additional amenity.

TISTED

The first main station layout was at Tisted. Here the navvies were to encounter the first major earthworks of the construction, as until now the route from Butts Junction was comparatively straightforward. Before the work had been under way long there were a few accidents and the first fatal one was to occur at East Tisted when on July 25th 1901 a lad named Arthur William Hankin, aged 15, sustained fatal injuries by being crushed between two ballast wagons. It was also at Privett that one unfortunate navvy suffered a terrible accident. After giving an engine driver some cheek, he was warned, "If you don't watch out, I'll run you over". Later that day he was in fact run over by the engine, severing both legs just below the knees. The unfortunate fellow was put onto a light engine and conveyed to Farringdon, all the while smoking his short pipe. The journey to Alton was continued by horse and wagon, only for him to be found dead on arrival at the hospital.

In line with the planning of the Meon Valley Railway with regard to its possible main line status, (the provision for long platforms and double track), the carefully and beautifully designed stations were a fine example of railway building at that time. Tisted was one of five such designs, three of which remain today, not for the reason they were intended, but retaining their usefulness in the 1980s, two as private houses.

The newly constructed railway, including splendid new bridges, were to make new scenes on the countryside.

Before mechanical methods were brought in, the horse and cart was to transport much of the spoil removed from the cuttings.

PRIVETT

From the moment the construction began, the line was climbing all the while to reach Privett which was the highest point, being 519 feet above sea level but at no greater ruling gradient than 1 in 100.

Privett station site.

Privett was the scene of some lengthy wrangling over the naming of the station, the L.S.W.R. insisted that because the station was in the parish of West Tisted it should be called so, while the owner of the land Mr. W.G. Nicholson of Basing Park, Privett was equally adamant that the station should be named Privett and threatened to withhold the transfer of the land unless he had his own way, and pointed out the confusion that might arise from having stations called East Tisted and West Tisted on the same railway line. In the end, Privett was the name that was to appear on the station name boards to the delight of the Nicholson family, and near the station a new Public House was built and called the "Privett Bush" with a wrought iron sign depicting a privett bush. Legend has it that the cost of the sign was £50, defrayed by Miss Isobel Nicholson.

PRIVETT XMAS 1899

Great rejoicing took place at the Navvy Mission on Boxing Day. The children assembled in the afternoon, and sat down to a splendid tea, which was admirably served by the workers and friends of the Mission. After the tea the parents of the children and about sixty navvy friends came in to amuse them, and witness the stripping of the Christmas tree. Almost everybody was the recipient of a warm and useful garment, and every child also received some useful toy. These were purchased by the voluntary contributions of their parents, which amounted to £1 16s.9d. and a generous gift of a handsomely dressed doll to every girl by Miss G. Nicholson of Basing Park. The garments were kindly sent by Mrs. Longman of Clifton, Mrs. Troller of Kettering, Miss Stewart of Limpsfield and Miss Nisbett of Wimbledon. The tree was kindly given by Mr. W. Nicholson. Mr. W. Turner of Privett gave a splendid lot of cakes and Mr. Fawley provided an ample supply of oranges and nuts. During the evening, Mr. D. Smith (the missionary) made an interesting speech. Speaking of the attendance at Sunday School, the children had put in about 70 per cent, and that they considered was very good considering the distance the children had to come. He was extremely grateful to all the friends and workers who had contributed to make the occasion such a delightful one. He then asked all present to show their appreciation by giving three hearty cheers. These were given in a right loyal way. The children dispersed about 8 o'clock, each receiving an orange and bun as they left the room.

Some of the navvies lived very close to the line!

The building of Privett Tunnel proved to be a testing time for everyone concerned, with a length of 1056 yards it was to produce volumes of chalk, indeed far more than had at first been estimated. The navvies at the southern end soon reached the Petersfield-Winchester road with the embankment but were held up for some considerable time by having to wait for the completion of the brick arch which was in fact a miniature road tunnel 167 feet in length, topped by a lofty embankment carrying the rails some 64 feet above the road.

This spot was the site of a large encampment of wooden huts on the northern side of the Petersfield-Winchester road and to the west of the railway embankment. These were to house the navvies with their wives and families – the site being chosen to be as near as possible to the largest earthworks on the whole railway.

Engineers plan the route at Privett tunnel.

A steam derrick used during the building of Privett tunnel.

Still a well-known landmark, this road tunnel on the A272, Winchester to Petersfield road, is seen here being constructed. Some reinforcement was used while the huge embankment above was gradually built up. Author's collection.

Some navvies and their families stand outside their temporary home.

PRIVETT TUNNEL

One of the most difficult tasks on the whole railway now confronted the navvies with the digging of Privett Tunnel, with yet more injuries and fatalities, two young navvies being seriously hurt in the deep cutting to the north of the tunnel, and one Richard Allen, aged 25, while engaged in 'trimming' trucks was caught by the end of one in the chest. He was put on a light engine to be conveyed to Farringdon but died of his injuries on the way to Alton. Yet another death occurred in the digging of the tunnel itself which is best described by quoting the newspaper report from the Hampshire Post of 27th January 1899.

"ACCIDENT PRIVETT TUNNEL"

**Shocking Accident on the new Railway
Two Men Buried Shocking Incidents**

A shocking accident has occurred on the works of the new railway between Fareham and Alton. In one of Mr. Nicholson's fields known by the name Little Collins Field, near the village of Privett some seven miles from Petersfield, a shaft which was the central one three of which were being bored in order to tunnel a hill, had been sunk about 40 feet when on Friday night working by the light of three candles, the sides fell in, and buried two men who were working at the bottom – James Owen a married man living at East Tisted and the other named George Brown aged 29 believed to be an Army Reserveman and to be single.

The shaft, which was 12 feet square, was to have been sunk to a depth of about 90 feet. The work had been in progress for several days, and on Friday night four men were engaged in the excavation by means of a steam crane. Two men were in the shaft, and the other two men were working at the top.

The night was very rough, and about midnight after some timber had been lowered to the men at the bottom of the shaft, the sides suddenly collapsed completely burying the two men. Information was immediately given to the foreman of the works and the police. Gangs of men set to work to dig out the earth. Mr. Relfe Jun. a member of the firm of contractors (Messrs. Relfe and Son of Plymouth) by whom the line is being constructed, was early in attendance on Saturday.

There was little hope that either of the men would get out alive but early on Monday morning a surprise was given to the workers.

About 5 o'clock when a depth of 20 feet had been reached, the man Owen was liberated. He was somewhat dazed and exhausted but he had received no bodily injuries whatsoever. He was at once taken to the house of Mr. Issac Stevens (foreman) of Sages Lane, Privett where he ate a good breakfast.

He afterwards went, with his wife and children, to his house, walking nearly all the way.

It appears that when the fall took place, the timbers above him fell crossways, and formed a protection from the slipping soil overhead. He was not hurt – but his mate was not so fortunate, and seems to have been crushed in the fall, so that he could not release himself. It is reported that Brown, after the fall, bade Owen farewell, and sent a message to his sister. Owen set to work, and with his hands and the help of a clasp knife, which he had on him, gradually worked his way upwards between the crossed pieces of timber until he reached the spot where he was found.

Owing to the way in which the timbers fell he had no difficulty in breathing.

After Owens liberation, the workmen continued digging until 10.30 a.m. on Wednesday morning, when the body of Brown was reached.

He was then quite dead.

An inquest was held yesterday (Thursday) in the School Room, Privett, the Jury returning a verdict of "accidental death".

ENTOMBED NAVVY'S PRAYER

Between January 20-22 1899 two men, named Brown and Owen, whilst sinking a shaft in connection with the Meon Valley Railway at Privett, were buried alive. Brown was killed, but Owen has lived to tell the tale of his terrible experience while buried under ground for over two days and two nights. The sides of the shaft, which was 40 feet deep, collapsed without warning. Brown was in the act of handing Owen a piece of wood when this took place. The manner in which the woodwork on the sides fell in left Owen free, and after all was quiet he commenced climbing. After climbing some way up Owen stopped, as Brown told him he was hemmed in and could not breathe. Owen cheered him by telling him he could hear the men working to get them out, but Brown, evidently knowing he had not long to live, tried to communicate his sister's address to Owen, afterwards bidding him good-bye, and saying the Lord's Prayer. Owen then heard a gurgling and gasping sound, and all communication ceased. With the aid of only a pocket-knife Owen dug his way upwards about twenty feet, letting the earth fall down the hole through which he came, until he was released on Monday morning by the rescue party, after an imprisonment of over fifty-three hours.

The unfortunate navvy, George Brown, who was killed in the accident at Privett Tunnel.

JUNCTION OF WEST MEON TUNNEL

A supper was held in the dining rooms of Lynch House on Tuesday of last week in celebration of the junction of the West Meon tunnel. Mr. Edward Ismay, cashier, presided, and there were about 50 present. After supper the Royal toast was drunk, and then the health of the firm, Messrs. R.T. Relf and Son. Mr. Ismay next proposed the health of Mr. Avery, the engineer, and Mr. Drayton, the tunnel foreman, and, in the course of his remarks, congratulated them on their successful work, and said he had been on public works for twenty years and had never seen a better junction. A tunnel on an acute curve is always a very difficult piece of work, and Mr. Avery and Mr. Drayton had made a junction within half an inch. The healths of Mr. Avery and Mr. Drayton were drunk with musical honours, and both suitably responded. The supper, supplied by Messrs. Beaten and Smyth went off splendidly, all the men enjoyed themselves, and there was plenty of singing. The evening closed with a vote of thanks to the chairman, proposed by Mr. Avery.

Occasionally they were allowed a rest!

Navvies and engineers standing outside the entrance of West Meon tunnel.

The worst "goings on" occurred at the West Meon Hut where drunken fights were commonplace. One very drunken navvy was stripped of his clothes and thrashed by his mates with stinging nettles. At "The White Horse", at West Meon, a tin hut was erected in the garden solely for the navvies use for drinking – they were so rowdy.

The deep cutting leading to Privett tunnel.

A new carriage drive was built from Privett Station to Basing House and the leftovers tipped on a large spoil bank to the north of the Railway Cottages at Privett. One more death is recorded during 1900 when Arthur Sunidge, labourer aged 23, died from injuries received in the Privett Tunnel when he and John Franklin were engaged in collecting empty trucks with an engine.

The tunnel was lighted only with candles, the men were riding the wagon farthermost from the engine, and as they bumped against an empty truck, Sunidge fell between the two trucks; a wheel passed over his body and he died later from his injuries.

The mammoth task of completing the tunnel proved to be a testing time for the navvies, foremen, overseers, and engineers whose job it had been to construct this tunnel some 1056 yards in length. The fatalities were to have a demoralising effect on the men and were to cause several to drift away to find other work even sometimes for less money, and with yet another tunnel just around the corner it was decided to bring more labour saving devices to the site in the form of steam excavators to make up the deficiency in the labour force.

The line was to descend now at a gradient of 1 in 100 and with West Meon Tunnel only half as long as Privett, the construction was to proceed fairly swiftly with surprisingly few injuries and none fatal.

A wagon full of chalk spoil, awaits removal from Privett tunnel.

Navvies hard at work, digging a cutting at West Meon.

The building of Privett tunnel, necessitated the lowering of horses through shafts, to the work area below. Even the men were lowered into the tunnel, by this means.

During the year 1900 the deaths of three men and two babies were recorded in the register at West Meon.

Buried in West Meon Church Yard
Jan 8th 1900 William Baxter Aged 45
Feb 12th 1900 Mark Westaway Aged 66
Dec 6th 1900 Joseph Doughty Aged 41

2 Babies

Apr 18th 1900 Frederick Simons Aged 3 months
Oct 20th 1900 William George Beech Aged 9 months.

All are buried in the western end of the top church yard – their address recorded simply as "Navvy Huts, West Meon".

Local landowners tried hard to stop their labourers going to work on the railway – the contractors paid more money than the farmers and in an effort to stop farm wages being pushed up, they threatened families with eviction from tied cottages if they had sons working on the railway, so that railway workers had to go and live with nearby relatives. At this point in the construction it is said that up to 600 men were engaged in building the Meon Valley Railway and inevitably there were tales of drunken fights.

At Woodlands near Privett the "Three Horseshoes" flourished as an Inn during this time but as the navvies moved on, the licence was transferred in 1901 to the new "Railway Hotel" at Droxford.

The entrance to Privett tunnel.

Navvies finishing off the embankments adjoining the viaduct.

WEST MEON VIADUCT

The line had now reached the river valley that was to give the railway its name, but to cross this valley an enormous viaduct was needed to carry the rails some 62 feet above the River Meon. The original plan was for a concrete viaduct with 8 arches, but due to soil conditions a revised plan for a 4 arch metal girder viaduct was put into being. The construction of the West Meon Viaduct was to use some 725 tons of steel, making four arches and estimated to cost £10,000. When it was completed people came from miles around to view it and four railway locomotives were placed, one on each span, to test the structure and its deflection: several schoolboys among the spectators, who watched until 2.30 p.m., were late for afternoon school and were caned.

Had the viaduct been built as originally intended, in concrete, perhaps it would not have been the first major item to be dismantled in 1956, because obviously being steel there was considerable value in the scrap. Ironically, all that now remains of the viaduct are the concrete bases for the pillars which were left behind by Thomas Ward, the scrap merchant, because they were worthless.

The site of the West Meon viaduct. This was originally to be an 8 arch concrete structure, but a 4 arch iron viaduct was to be favoured because of soil conditions.

By the time West Meon was reached, these mechanical methods were employed to help speed up construction.

This traction engine was used, to pull some of the heavier loads.

WEST MEON

A very deep cutting gave access to the site of West Meon Station. The station house was constructed to the same standard design as those built already at Tisted and Privett, namely of brick, faced with Portland stone. The 600 foot long platforms were able to accommodate ten coach trains on a through route from Waterloo to Gosport to connect with the Stokes Bay Isle of Wight steamer service and it was hoped that Queen Victoria might use this route to Osborne House, but of course Her Majesty died before the opening of the railway.

So far, the building of this new railway had brought prosperity to the public houses with record sales of beer, wine, bread, cheese and pickles and of course many were to do board and lodging. One such was the New Inn, West Meon, where the tenant Mrs. Ann Stone, assisted by her son William, was to lodge several railway navvies especially during the building of the West Meon Viaduct, when legend has it that no sooner had the day shift left for work after breakfast, than the night shift was to arrive and jump into the same beds! Also to prosper during this time were the local horse owners. Farmer Edwards of Cleverley Farm, West Meon was said to have worked 90 consecutive days with horse and cart conveying bricks for the building of West Meon tunnel.

Also in great demand were the local water carts which were needed to convey water for the concrete and cement needed to build the bridges. Other building materials were brought to the sites by traction engines some of which towed three wagons.

At West Meon a deep well was sunk to provide water to a water tower to be installed at West Meon Station – indeed when the railway was opened this was the only watering point for the locomotives between Alton and Fareham. The storage tank was situated just above the railway cottages at West Meon.

After West Meon the going was fairly easy. The long embankment from West Meon to Meonstoke passed, for the most part, through the property of W. Woods Esq. who resided at Warnford Park. At Peake Farm several small culverts were made to carry under the railway the small streams that rise on the eastern side of the line into the water meadows and into the River Meon.

So far, the railway had followed almost continually the old London to Gosport coach road, and was in fact to do so over almost its entire length.

West Meon station, very nearly ready for the opening day.

Huge amounts of chalk were excavated to form the cuttings.

The chalk dug from the cuttings was used to make the embankments.

DROXFORD

At Droxford a deep cutting gave access to the station which was to be the scene of some interesting discoveries Soon after the station area was commenced a skeleton was unearthed. The police were called and for a while all work was halted whilst the authorities investigated the possibility of a murder case. The skeleton was eventually established to be of Anglo Saxon origin and as more skeletons were unearthed it was obvious that a burial ground had been discovered. Several objects were found in the graves, among the more interesting were an iron belt buckle inlaid with silver wire, a pair of gilded bronze brooches, the bronze binder of a bucket and several weapons such as spear tips and arrow heads.

Droxford Cemetery 1900

A local antiquary, William Dale, then of 5 Sussex Place, Southampton, visited the site, having been informed that human bones and pieces of iron work had been found, and retrieved a number of objects which were subsequently identified as Anglo Saxon by Mr. Charles Read of the British Museum.

During the summer of 1900 and the autumn and winter of 1901-02, Dale visited the site regularly and was able, with the help of "a couple of navvies who were more intelligent than was usual with their class", to retrieve a quantity of objects and bones, which were presented to the British Museum.

After the line had been made, the site was widened to accommodate the platform, station buildings, and goods yard, during which a further number of objects were found. These were presented to the City Museum, Winchester.

William Dale evidently spent a considerable amount of time on the site, but apart from two published notes, no written record of his observations has been traced in any of the

Carpenters pose during a break in the construction of Droxford Station. John Bosworth.

archives held by the more important Libraries, Museums and Record Offices in Hampshire.

The Hampshire Chronicle records have been scanned for references to the cemetery for the period during which the cutting was made at Droxford, but no direct references occur, and it is also somewhat surprising that the work on the line went almost unnoticed in the local press. Although the site had been noted for its archaelogical interest, it was to be 1974 before it was extensively excavated and more skeletons discovered.

Droxford was also the scene of the building of the new "Railway Hotel" whose licence had been transferred from "The Horseshoes" at Woodlands. The station site at Droxford was to cut right through the existing road to Soberton so that a completely new road was made to pass in front of the station forecourt and was appropriately named Station Road.

A busy scene with, it is thought, locomotive No. 11.

From Droxford onwards the railway ran through the centre of the valley immediately beside the River Meon so that the contractors knew they were to experience a sudden and dramatic change in the soil formation ahead at Soberton.

At Selworth Lane began the "Reading Beds", a peculiar mixture of clay and stones which was to give trouble over almost the entire life of the Meon Valley Line. At Hookers Dene there was to be continual slipping of the embankment, the worst occurring in 1946 when major restoration took place. It was here that an iron bar and a sleeper chair for leverage were hidden in the long grass to allow the gangers to lift and pack the sleepers, a job that needed doing frequently.

A photograph, of another photographer recording the building of the railway.

MISLINGFORD

A clay cutting at Mislingford also gave trouble on this difficult stretch of line, defying all other attempts, it was eventually stabilised by the use of chalk "groynes" for drainage and the building of a low concrete retaining wall to arrest the flow of clay onto the track during wet weather.

Inclement weather, coupled with the difficult soil formation held up work for some considerable time, time enough in fact for the L.S.W.R. to announce that the opening of the line would not now take place in March 1903 as planned, but would probably be at some later date, possibly not until some time in June.

WICKHAM

The line now had to cross the River Meon towards the site of Wickham Station and after it, a large steel structure supported on cylindrical piers was needed to bridge the river yet again, where the Meon was some 30 feet wide in places. From now on the embankment grew shallower and shallower, eventually to run firstly through

Once Droxford was passed, the awkward soil of the "Reading Beds" was reached near Meonstoke. John Bosworth.

The navvies pose at a point near Wickham. John Bosworth.

The construction of the bridge at Wickham spanning the River Meon. John Bosworth.

The spire of Wickham Church is visible, at the bridge site. John Bosworth.

Looking like a Model – Wickham station, soon after construction.

0-4-0ST "Blanche" near Wickham.

Believed to be 0-4-0ST "R.T. Relf & Son No. 11".

Building a bridge in the Forest of Bere.

Laying the foundations to one of the bridges.

Fareham tunnels taken between September 1906 and June 1907, with major repairs well under way. The line was closed during this period, rail traffic used the deviation line. C.K. Saunders collection.

flat open fields, within sound of trains on the Bishopstoke to Gosport line which the Meon Valley was to join at Knowle, and then through the notorious Fareham tunnels which had given so much trouble since 1841 when cutting through the ridge running westwards from Portsdown to the valley of the Meon, the contractors encountered a soil that defied description. When dry, the soil had to be blasted to dig the cuttings and yet after rain it became little better than fluid mud.

Thomas Brassey, the engineering contractor, and his men, had toiled trying one idea after another – retaining walls were erected to try and contain the cutting slopes in the tunnel approaches, but during the first spell of wet weather the soil just spewed over the parapets and onto the rails.

Great concern was felt for the stability of the tunnel, and indeed after four days running the Chief Engineer, Joseph Locke, took fright and closed the line temporarily.

Despite these problems, Meon Valley trains were to run from Knowle Junction to Fareham using the existing main line from Bishopstoke. But from 2nd Oct 1904 a tunnel deviation line, built on the land acquired originally for the Meon Valley route (Railway No. 1) and single line only, was used for all up trains to Alton and Bishopstoke. All down trains used the tunnel line, which was also singled at this time. From September 1906, while the tunnels received major repairs, the deviation line was doubled and all trains used this route. Once repairs were completed in June 1907, a single line was opened through the tunnels to carry all up and down Meon Valley trains, there being no connections at Knowle at all. With the run completed, the new Meon Valley Railway was ready for the opening.

A rumour went round at the time that part of its cost was funded by the War Office and was smuggled through the estimates because the Army Chiefs of Staff had found that during the Boer War the rail communications between the large encampments at Aldershot and the South Coast were very poor, and they were anxious to have an extra rail link to the ports.

A drainage culvert is visible in this view.

The five stations, operated by its own stationmaster, three signalmen, porters and office staff, had accommodation for dealing with horses, livestock and carriages. Quite large sidings for goods traffic were also provided at Farringdon and at Mislingford. 5 ton capacity cranes were erected at each of the stations.

The siding at Mislingford, situated between Droxford and Wickham, could only be shunted by an "up" goods train, because the points were facing for down trains, and were operated from a ground frame and controlled by the tablet for the section. When it was necessary for the rear part of the goods train to be left on the running line, the guard in charge was to securely brake the train before the engine was detached. This part of the line was on a gradient of 1 in 90 falling towards Wickham and was the only section of the Meon Valley Line where the ruling gradient was less than 1 in 100.

March 20th 1903

At Alresford Brewster Sessions, A.F. Downie, Solicitor of Alton, applied on behalf of M. and W. Nicholson for a provisional licence for a new public house proposed to be built in the parish of West Tisted, near Privett Station on the Meon Valley Railway. The application really meant the transfer from the New Inn, West Tisted, to a new house to be called The Privett Bush. The old house has been cut right away from the main road by the new Railway. Bench granted the new licence.

MEON VALLEY RAILWAY WORKS – 1900

"Peter Lombard" or Canon Benham, who is well known as a native of West Meon, writes as follows in the Church Times:-

One goes on enlarging one's experience. Much as I have travelled in the course of my life, I never till this week saw a railway in the course of making. A charming scene of hill and dale, cornfield and wood, once as familiar to me as Cheapside is now, where I have rambled as a boy, picking nuts or birds' nesting, to-day having a new line of the South Western Railway making right through it. Much of the beauty must of necessity be destroyed but it would be idle to complain of that. I trust that the people will have reason to rejoice in the benefit. And the great chalk embankments, now as ugly as they can be, will soften down and be clothed in green, and probably planted with trees. And I shall be able, if living, to run down in an hour or two to my native village, instead of having to go twelve miles over a rather rough road, as I used to do of yore, to the nearest railway station. I started from that village some years ago, at half-past seven one winter's morning, and was duly deposited in a third-class carriage at Winchester, which then rumbled along, stopping at every station, and I got to London but a very short time before evening set in.

It is curious and interesting to see the works going on. There are cuttings through the rising ground, and a vast amount of chalk is brought forth to level up the valley beyond. It looks all simple enough when you contemplate a finished line, and see the trains gliding so swiftly and easily over it, but see it in course of construction, and what a prodigious work it is. I stood and watched the big carts coming out of the cuttings and along the chalk road already constructed; by some ingenious construction which I might have understood had I climbed up sixty feet, these carts at a given point wheeled round, shot their load out on to the heap, and went back for more. 'Da capo'. The heap looked no bigger for the addition. I wonder how many cart loads it takes to bridge that little valley over.

But yet more interesting by far are the 'living agents'. The 'navvies' swarm in the streets of the quiet village, and it is a pleasure to have to write that the people like them and their ways so far as I gathered. What is a navvy? The name, I find, originated along with the Bridgewater canals. When these were made all over England to increase the water traffic the diggers were called the 'navigators' because their were increasing the navigation and the name has since got fixed upon the kindred occupation of railway-making. Perhaps it was because their clothes were rough fustian, and their boots muddy, and their limbs stalwart, that the opinion got spread abroad that they were one and all brutalised fighters. Good Miss Marsh – whose name I have just been looking for in vain in the Dictionary of National Biography – taught the British people what fine fellows some of these navvies can be. And she has thereby gained a most honoured name in literature. There they were, as decent fellows as need be so far as I saw; huts are scattered about all over the landscape, like the coops in a pheasant preserve, and here they will sojurn till the road is finished.

When they came swarming into the place, Dibbs, the general dealer, thought it a time to put up his prices at once, but it didn't answer, for Goahead and Brisk, two enterprising fellows, took a big house and converted it into a store as well as a restaurant, and they are hard at work with their spec. The squire took me over the place, and it was very interesting. First we went into a quondam stable, now converted into a bakehouse. There is an enormous machine, capable (so the attendant told us) of baking 3000 2lb. loaves a day. Then we went into another room wherein were hanging a vast number of joints of meat. The general result is summed up in the fact that a good dinner of meat, vegetables and bread can be supplied for sixpence, and a pint of wholesome beer with it for twopence. A good many of them are total abstainers and there was a perfect army of bottles of beverages to suit them. We went through the stores – stationery, clothing, groceries, even skipping ropes for children – I saw all these things as I walked through. There are carts which go a round of fifteen miles a day to the several centres of navvy labour to carry the bread and meat. Altogether a very pleasant visit, and I am looking forward in hope of another run down when the line shall be finished.

A typical navvy with his family.

Looking north and believed to be the opening week of the Meon Valley Railway at West Meon station, in June 1903. Note 'West Meon' painted on the platform barrows, and streamer adorning the tracks. Author's collection.

OPENING 1st JUNE 1903

An original opening date of 25th March 1903 was delayed, due to there being various signalling and track works remaining to be completed, especially at the Alton end. Curiously enough there is no record of any official opening ceremony, in fact the only merrymaking that took place occurred in the large country houses adjacent to the line – one such large luncheon party was held in Warnford House, the home of William Woods, with a ride on the new railway during the afternoon as a bonus. The opening day was a Whit Monday and a Bank Holiday, so that lots of people whose only mode of transport until now had been the horse and carriage, had the day off work to see the railway which was still an innovation in rural areas.

For the first ride on the Meon Valley Railway, one was allowed a free ride to the next station, whereupon one had the choice of paying the fare back by the next train to ones starting point, or at worst, walking!

Anyone choosing to walk home would have had a journey of 5 miles between any two stations. The service at first consisted of six passenger trains each way from Monday to Saturday and two trains each way on Sunday; there was an extra late train on Saturday evenings for people travelling for instance from Portsmouth. There were several excursions to the sea on summer Sundays, the trains originating from such places as Aldershot, Woking and Ascot and these were pretty well patronised.

Waterloo to Gosport through trains were mostly hauled by Adams "Jubilee" Class 0-4-2 locomotives and the Alton-Fareham only were firstly Adams 4-4-2 Radial Tanks – the engines were turned on the "triangle" at Gosport and at Alton a turntable was provided.

Here is a view of the very first train on Monday June 1st 1903 hauled by an unidentified Adams Radial 4-4-2T. Author's collection.

HAMPSHIRE TELEGRAPH AND POST, JUNE 5, 1903

On Monday the London and South Western Railway Company opened for traffic what is known as the Meon Valley Railway.

The new railway has been designed and constructed to form a portion of a main through line of railway from London to Portsmouth, Stokes Bay, and also to Southampton via Netley. It is 22¼ miles long, and commences by a junction with the South Western Company's Alton and Winchester branch line near Alton, and connects at the other end with the Company's Eastleigh and Portsmouth branch line at Knowle, about 2 miles north of Fareham. The ruling gradient is one in 100, and all the curves are suitable for running at express speed. The earthwork and permanent way are single, but the tunnels, viaduct, and most of the under bridges are constructed for a double line of railway. There are five stations on the line, and the platforms are all 600 ft. in length, so as to be available for main line trains, by which the line will ultimately be used. The permanent way is of the heaviest South Western type, fully-ballasted, and the signals are of the most approved pattern. The line passes through a lovely country, rich in literary and historical associations. About a mile from Alton it passes through the village of Chawton, where close to the line stands the house in which Jane Austen wrote several of her novels. Further south a fine view is obtained of Gilbert White's country passing the village of Farringdon, where he often preached; and near the famous Hanger at East Tisted the first station on the line is reached. This is the nearest railway station to the historic village, a short walk across the highland bringing into view the 'straggling street', which still possesses much of its old-world charm. The next station is at Privett, where a tunnel 1056 yards long has been cut through the chalk formation. West Meon, famous in history as the site of a battle between the Royalists (under Sir William Waller) and the Cavaliers in 1644, is reached through another tunnel 539 yards long. Here also the country is of great interest to the archaeologist, for on Old Winchester Hill, which stands 662 ft. high on the right of the line, is what has been described as "a mighty prehistoric camp".At West Meon the railway crosses the River Meon at a height of 62 ft. on a viaduct of 4 arches, each of 56 ft span, and enters the "Sweet Meon land". There is a station at Droxford - near is Hambledon, of early cricket memory - and the line continues its course to Knowle along the bank of the river. The line will no doubt serve to develop the fruit-growing industry of that neighbourhood. Messrs. R.T. Relf & Son of Plymouth, were the contractors and the line has taken over 3 years to construct. There was no opening ceremony on Monday.

One person fortunate in being able to travel on the first and last day of this passenger service, was a local resident, Miss H.M. Smith. Here she is being greeted by the Assistant District Traffic Superintendent, Mr. R. Shervington of Alton. Author's collection.

A very early early view of Alton station, with what is thought to be a T9 heading a through Waterloo to Gosport train. (Pre-1914).

The last remaining L12 4-4-0 No. 30434 gets away from Alton on 4th April 1953 with a southbound Meon Valley freight. Pamlin Prints, Croydon.

Alton Goods Staff prior to the Second World War; Bill Linott, Ron Wiltshire, Mr. Johnson, Len Pain, Ted Mayne, Mr. Gubell and Stan Lawford. Author's collection.

In British Rail days, Len Hillier gives the right of way to Charlie Arthur, the guard of a departing Alton train. Author's collection.

The signal box at Butts Junction south of Alton, has a good view of the three lines under its control, this ceased to operate after 1937. Author's collection.

The remains of Butts Junction in January 1983. It is difficult to judge now the direction of the three lines separating at Butts, although the track straight ahead can just be seen. This will hopefully see continued traffic, once the Mid-Hants Railway extends its line from Medstead to Alton. Note all that is left of the signal box. R.C. Hardingham.

This metal bridge at Butts Junction, was widened to accommodate the Meon Valley Railway in early days of its construction. It is pictured here in January 1983. R.C. Hardingham.

With the Mid-Hants Railway in the background, 700 Class No. 30698 works a short freight from Alton to Farringdon in 1956 after closure of the middle section. E.C. Griffith.

The first months of the new railways life, saw it settle down to a fairly busy time, goods traffic being the main source of revenue.

The lower half of the line ran through an extensive market gardening area, from which produce was despatched to various parts of the country in box vans, whilst "strawberry specials" were run during the season with whole trains of strawberries being loaded at Mislingford and Wickham.

Milk was brought in churns to all stations by horse and cart for despatch to Portsea Island Co-Op dairy, milk vans being attached to the normal passenger services, and livestock travelled frequently to and from markets at Alton and Fareham.

Each station had at least one Coal Merchant, West Meon having no less than three; one Issac Abram operated from both Privett and West Meon.

So great was the popularity of Alton Market in 1908, the railway company issued special market tickets from the surrounding area, and one could get a ticket to Alton on Tuesdays from Fareham for 2s.9d., West Meon for 1s.4d., Privett for 11d. and Tisted for 7d.

With the Meon Valley line now in full swing, and the Basingstoke-Alton line having opened two years previously, the Butts Junction was to see great activity, the signal box having to deal with trains from four directions. Legend has it that on many occasions the signalman there cooked his breakfast, but never had time to eat it!

West Meon was the scene of whole farms arriving by rail from such far away places as Cumberland and Northumberland, having hired

Q1 class 0-6-0 No. 33020 coasts through Alton station with a Farringdon goods train. T. Wright.

The steel bridge which crossed the road at Hedge Corner caused some problems when the time came for it to be dismantled. The foreman of Thomas Ward, one Fred Long, asked the police if they might close the A32 for a day whilst the bridge was being taken down. The reply was, no and nor could traffic be held up by traffic lights. So the men of Thomas Ward began the task of cutting up the bridge piece by piece. All went well until the time came for the crane to take the weight of the main section released. The crane driver realised that the piece was too heavy and let the whole thing drop rather suddenly onto the remainder of the bridge, causing it to dip in the middle. Traffic was held up for a considerable time whilst the men removed the pieces! M. Gunner.

Farringdon looking north towards Butts Junction. This one coach length platform was provided for local residents in May 1931. Author's collection.

special trains to do so. At the time of writing, sons and grandsons of those farmers still own land bought by their ancestors from the North of England.

With the outbreak of the First World War the Meon Valley line was used for the passage of troop trains bound for the docks and France, but during this time came the withdrawal of the Waterloo to Gosport through services which in fact were never fully restored. It was hoped that the end of the war would see the second track being laid as the Admiralty had expressed some interest in the line as a strategic route, but it never came to anything.

The line never prospered, attaining only the status of a rural branch line and only as a Hampshire railway backwater in the years to come. The trains got shorter and shorter, from four and six coach trains, down to the two coach push-pull sets, which meant that trains ran back and forth from Alton to Fareham without the need to turn the locomotives. These sets were usually worked by M7 0-4-4 Tank engines, which looked rather forlorn standing alongside platforms some 600 feet long originally intended for 10 coach trains.

An event which is worthy of note took place during the 1920's: in the minutes of the Corhampton Parish Meeting it is recorded: "That this meeting requests the L.S.W.R. to provide a halt or siding at Pound Lane, in the Parish of Meonstoke, for the convenience of the residents in the three adjoining parishes of Meonstoke, Exton and Corhampton and which will assist the local farmers in the transport of milk etc. to the towns". Meonstoke Parish Meeting passed a similar resolution. This proposal was given some consideration but never received approval. The site of the Meonstoke siding was marked very early in the life of the line by a short piece of rail let into the ground, which remained in situ until 1960, when it wrecked a grass cutting machine belonging to an unsuspecting hay making farmer.

The 1920's saw ever increasing competition from the fast developing internal combustion engine, with more and more commercial vehicles appearing and making serious inroads into the railways revenue, by competing with them for the carriage of goods, by offering door to door service at favourable rates.

Farringdon Goods siding was controlled from this wooden cabin, to the north of the platform. M. Gunner.

A road bridge at Farringdon in January 1983 after nature has taken over, quite a contrast to a similar view on page 46. R.C. Hardingham.

Ex-LSWR M7 No. 54 leaves Farringdon for Alton. Some years later in BR days the same locomotive, but now as No. 30054, takes a similar afternoon train. E.C. Griffith.

Tisted, also the station for Selborne, viewed from the north. Lens of Sutton.

A general view of Tisted station. Lens of Sutton.

In the last week of passenger train operation M7 No. 30054, a regular on the line, prepares to depart from Tisted with the 11.56 from Fareham to Alton, on 29th Jan 1955. S.C. Nash.

A view looking north showing Tisted and its LSWR water tank. M. Gunner.

Accelerating away from Tisted with a tremendous smoke screen, is M7 No. 30055 with a northbound train. T. Wright.

Auto set No. 4 with 30054 at the rear, about to depart from Tisted. T. Wright.

A loco crew pose for the camera at Tisted in 1947. E.C. Griffith.

Two of the staff, Harry Appleton and Jimmy Bullen proud to be photographed at Tisted in 1954. Author's collection.

Tisted signal box in 1956. M. Gunner.

Tisted station from the south, in an overgrown state. Lens of Sutton.

The route of the line looking north is clearly seen at Tisted station, now a private dwelling. R.C. Hardingham.

The magnificent architecture of the railway stations on the line, now makes an attractive purchase for a country home. January 1983. R.C. Hardingham.

In a typical Meon Valley Railway setting, M7 No. 30480 approaches Privett station in 1950. E.C. Griffith.

Privett station looking south from the A32 roadbridge. Lens of Sutton.

Privett signal box dominates this photograph of Privett station looking north. Author's collection.

The neat construction is shown of Privett signal box, which ceased to be used for conventional signalling in 1922. M. Gunner.

In 1949 L12 No. 30420 coasts through Privett station with an Alton goods. E.C. Griffith.

Although during the summer months there were many Sunday excursion trains to the sea running down the Meon Valley line , by trains originating from Ascot and Farnham, in the years which followed the 1914-1918 War, it had become quite clear that there was to be no massive increase in passenger revenue and therefore no real need for a very frequent train service, or for the doubling of the track. From that time economies began to be made. During 1922 the "UP" line at Privett ceased to be used by "UP" passenger trains and Privett signal box ceased to be a block post.

From the day the signals were taken out of use at Privett, the down line became the running line for both up and down trains, the up line was reduced to siding status, but had to be kept because access to the long siding was from that line.

Trap points were installed at the Alton end of the up line under the A32 road bridge to prevent any runaway wagons from blocking the main running line, and the old up line appears to have been used for infrequent shunting movements right up to the closure in February 1955, the last time being in the last week the line was open when some coaches, which had been stored in the long siding, were removed.

The alterations at Privett meant that with no signals to maintain, signalmen could be transferred elsewhere. The footbridge was no longer needed and with the signalbox converted to a ground frame and no lighting provided for the up platform, Privett must have been considerably cheaper to run. The changes also meant that Tisted to West Meon was the new block section and with new tablet machines and a new tablet to unlock the ground frame at Privett installed, the bell code between Tisted and West Meon was repeated at Privett, so that staff there knew when a train was due. The warning bell being situated under the platform awning, near the booking office.

The distant signals were left at Privett to become "marker lights" showing a white light to let train drivers know they were approaching the station. The points leading into Privett Goods Yard had now become facing points to up trains and had to be fitted with a facing point lock. At about this time the footbridges at Tisted, Wickham

Class 700 No. 30325 shunts the Privett goods. S.C. Nash.

For the best kept section of line at Privett in 1950, the permanent way gang at the time, received a diploma from Mr. V.A.M. Robertson, Chief Civil Engineer, Southern Region. Author's collection.

The space once occupied by trains at Privett now accommodates a fishpond, at this privately owned house. January 1983. R.C. Hardingham.

Privett tunnel. M. Gunner.

and West Meon were taken down. A break was made in the platforms, near the signal box and a foot crossing made with sleepers, so that passengers could cross the line under the signalman's "watchful eye". These alterations came into use in June 1926.

The festive season of 1927 will long be remembered by railwaymen, Christmas Day, Boxing Day and the following two days saw what was described as the greatest snowstorm in living memory, which disrupted railway communications, particularly in Hampshire, where snow began to fall at about 6 p.m. on Christmas Day and continued unceasingly for the following two days, accompanied by a bitter wind of great velocity, so that the Meon Valley line had deep drifts at Farringdon, Privett and West Meon.

December 27th began with shrieking winds and blinding snow. The 5.40 Waterloo to Gosport (probably a through service laid on for the Christmas holiday) became stuck in a huge drift near Tisted, which completely blocked the Meon Valley line. Gangs of workmen were to take twenty four hours before clearing a way for train services to be resumed.

In May 1931, the Southern Railway added a timber platform at Farringdon, hitherto only a goods depot, following a request from local inhabitants for passenger trains to call. Passengers intending to alight at Farringdon Halt were asked to travel in the coach nearest the engine, the platform being only one coach length and originally named Farringdon Platform in May 1932, but renamed Farringdon on July 8th 1934.

In 1937 the Southern Railways' electrification scheme was to see electric trains operating from Waterloo only to Alton and not as it was hoped, down the valley to Fareham. This scheme had seemed the last chance of ever seeing the laying of the second track to make the Meon Valley line once more a through route, but this was not to be and the original idea of making all bridges and tunnels wide enough for two tracks, was all for nothing.

Nearing West Meon tunnel, L12 No. 30420 picks up speed with a West Meon freight train in 1949. E.C. Griffith.

To carry the rails of the Meon Valley line some 62 feet above the River Meon and road to East Meon, this huge construction of 725 tons of steel was erected just north of West Meon station. Author's collection.

Just coming off the West Meon viaduct is M7 No. 30054 with its train for Alton. Southern Newspapers Ltd.

Station staff and permanent way men pose while caring for their well kept station. Author's collection.

In this south view, the footbridge dominates West Meon station. Author's collection.

A rare postcard view shows West Meon station from the road bridge. Note the newly excavated banks of the cutting to the north. Author's collection.

West Meon station clearly in operation with a Fareham bound train preparing for departure. Author's collection.

The T9 Class were well associated with the Meon Valley Railway. Here we have a splendid example with No. 30708 in charge of a northbound freight at West Meon station in 1949. E.C. Griffith.

General view of West Meon station and freight yard, with an L12 performing its duties in 1950. P.M. Alexander.

Approaching West Meon, 700 Class No. 30325 in fine fettle with the 12.23 Fareham to Alton freight train on 4th Dec. 1954. S.C. Nash.

Well known photographer of the area, Mr. Edward Griffith, stands on the footplate of Q Class No. 545 at West Meon station in 1947.

At West Meon station in 1948, Driver Farley of Guildford and Guard Len Pain, look pleased to be in the company of T9 No. 732 still in its Southern livery. Author's collection.

Framed in the archway of the road bridge at West Meon station, an up goods train trundles through the platforms. Southern Newspapers Ltd.

The same view over twenty eight years later, on 20th January 1983. R.C. Hardingham.

Just prior to closure, George Jackson of the railway staff surveys the West Meon station scene in 1955. The News, Portsmouth.

The author second from left, stands with fellow workers while preparing to collect the last delivery of coal brought in by rail. Note author's coal lorry in the background. Author's collection.

No more trains for West Meon, with demolition underway. Hugh Davies.

West Meon signal box after closure. M. Gunner.

The day after official closure, an RCTS special train headed by T9s Nos. 30301 and 30732 pause for refreshment at West Meon station, marking the final sad demise of a very special railway. T. Wright.

On the 15th May 1960, West Meon station has lost all but its railway building, this also with time, would eventually be demolished, leaving nature to devour the platforms unhindered. T. Wright.

THE SECOND WORLD WAR

The Second World War was to follow in less than two years, and this was to delay very effectively most of the railway improvements and schemes in general, not only those in the Meon Valley. For a time most railway lines were to experience extra traffic, mostly in the form of troop trains, which ran late at night, or on Sundays; almost from the outbreak of war, a box van was added to all Meon Valley trains to cater for extra parcels and troops' luggage.

The Luftwaffe also thought that this part of the world ought to receive some attention, a Junkers 88 dropped bombs at Droxford Station, causing light damage to the station buildings, but demolishing two of the station cottages. The aircraft flew on down the valley dropping bombs both sides of the line at Soberton, but missing the track altogether. At West Meon Station, two coalmen, weighing coal for W. Stone, dived for cover upon realising the plane was a "Jerry". However, the object of his attentions proved to be the West Meon tunnel and a bomb was dropped aiming for the northern portal, fortunately it missed, but blew up several yards of track and sleepers and damaged Vinnells Lane bridge. Frantic telephone calls were made to Privett Station, thankfully in time to halt the 4.30 ex-Alton down passenger train, so avoiding, what could have been, a serious accident. Workmen soon repaired the track and normal train services were resumed.

Various extra traffic movements took place during the war time which helped to break the monotony of the day to day workings of the Meon Valley line. In 1941 a special military train travelled from Swallowcliffe to Droxford, to experiment in the movement, by rail, of troops and vehicles together. The train consisted of a Drummond 700 class "Black Motor", hauling six coaches, loaded with troops and 35 Bren Gun Carriers, loaded on flat bogie wagons. The train stayed two days in the long siding, before moving off to the coast, after being delayed several hours by vacuum trouble. Another such special train arrived late one evening at Tisted. This was shunted into the long siding for the night. The driver and fireman had received instructions to draw the fire for the night, but to be ready with a good head of steam at daylight and to move off. Two days later staff were to learn, that the contents of the wagons were 48 Sea Mines destined for the British Channel.

The Railways' shining hour though, was to come on Thursday June 2nd 1944. The long siding at Droxford Station was chosen to be the place where a special train, containing the War Cabinet, would stay for a few days, whilst final preparations were made for the D Day invasion in Normandy.

Although Wickham would have been nearer to the S.H.A.P.E. H.Q. at Southwick House, more cover was provided at Droxford by virtue of the station lying in a cutting and also having a thick belt of beech trees on the north side. The decision followed a rejection of a proposal put forward by the United States Army, to build a branch line from the Meon Valley Line, into the hills near Southwick. No advance information was given as to the departure and arrival time, other than a telephone call from each tablet section, for all other trains to clear the main line to allow passage of a special train. The special train, upon arrival at Droxford, proved to be the L.M.S. Royal Train, six gleaming red coaches hauled by a Drummond T9. A spare engine was

Reg Gould, who was Porter/Signalman at Droxford during the "D-Day" period. Author's collection.

Left to right; Mr. Mackenzie King, (Canada) Mr. Winston Churchill, (Great Britain) Mr. Peter Fraser, (New Zealand) General Eisenhower, (U.S.A.) Sir G. Huggins (S. Rhodesia) and General Smuts, (S. Africa) – standing in front of their special train. Although this is reputed to have been taken at Droxford, the design of the station canopy clearly illustrates that in fact it was elsewhere on the South Coast. This photograph used to hang in the booking hall at Droxford.

to remain in the yard for emergencies, as was a mess van. The H.Q. Inspector from Waterloo was in attendance throughout the stay at Droxford.

The Station was heavily guarded, troops being volunteers drawn from the many army camps stationed in Hampshire at that time and changed every four hours. A private telephone line was laid on and tight security was maintained. When the occupants of the train wished to leave the station, instructions were shouted to the engine crew, who then drew the train into the up platform with everyone going out through the booking hall to the waiting staff cars, with the exception of Churchill, who insisted on going out through the goods yard.

During these two notable days in the life of Droxford and the Meon Valley Railway, there were, at some time during those momentous discussions, Mr. Mackenzie King, Mr. Peter Frazer, Sir Godfrey Huggins, General Smuts, General Eisenhower, General de Gaulle, Mr. Anthony Eden, Mr. Ernest Bevin and Air Marshal Tedder. The village says that it was here that the decision to postpone "Overlord" (the codeword for the invasion) was taken.

On Sunday June 5th the special train left Droxford at 6.58 p.m. The 5.56 p.m. Portsmouth to Woking train had been shunted into the long siding at Tisted to allow the "train" to pass on its way back to Waterloo. The watching railway staff were unaware that the following day would see the commencement of the invasion of Europe.

Droxford station looking south. Lens of Sutton.

Droxford station looking north. G.P. Gardiner collection.

An early 1920s view of Droxford station, with an interesting LSWR notice board advertising far distant places in those days, to such resorts as Swanage and Lyme Regis. Author's collection.

Droxford signalman awaits the stopping of M7 No. 30055, to hand the driver the token for the approaching single section north to West Meon. T. Wright.

With all eyes to the left and the home starter signal in the off position, an Alton train is seen leaving Droxford in Feb 1955. The News, Portsmouth.

All was quiet until T9 No. 30726 was seen heading the 10.20am Alton to Fareham goods by the Droxford signalman, in the last week of full operations. The News, Portsmouth.

Approaching Droxford (for Hambledon) M7 No. 30055 brings in the 2.48 Fareham to Alton train on 4th Dec 1954. S.C. Nash.

Station staff and engine crew come together, for a photograph of one of the last departing trains from Droxford. The News, Portsmouth.

Inside Droxford signal box. Author's collection.

Droxford staff discuss the days traffic outside the signal box in Southern Railway days. Author's collection.

An unidentified U Class 2-6-0 is being guided into Droxford yard with that days goods train. L.J. Dommett.

Shunting at Droxford yard. L.J. Dommett.

Porter at Droxford. L.J. Dommett.

BR 4MT Class 2-6-0 No. 76059 is seen here running around its goods train at Droxford, after arrival from Fareham. D. Fereday Glenn.

Little has changed to the structure of the front of Droxford station. But the building and surrounding railway area, is now used for lorry driver training and tuition. January 1983. R.C. Hardingham.

After the activity of the Second World War and latter day preservation schemes, the canopy and station survive at Droxford in January 1983. R.C. Hardingham.

In the last years of operation, an unidentified U Class 2-6-0 is seen passing Mislingford goods siding. M. Gunner.

Hurrying through the Forest of Bere, is U Class No. 31808 approaching Mislingford with a goods train bound for Droxford. D. Fereday Glenn.

Not a train in sight in this view of Wickham station looking south on the 31st May 1952. Pamlin Prints, Croydon.

Wickham station with all signals at danger, looking north. Lens of Sutton.

An Adams tank engine with five coaches in an early view of Wickham station in LSWR days.

Unidentified M7 departing Wickham for Droxford in 1954. Author's collection.

With an array of rails to the fore, an Alton train gets away from Wickham in 1954. Author's collection.

With steam in abundance M7 No. 30055 awaits departure from Wickham with a train for Alton on the last day, 5th Feb 1955. Lens of Sutton.

Stationmaster Mr. W.F. Squire and Mr. A. Swatton stand outside Wickham signal box, in the early 1950s. Author's collection.

Wrapped up for a cold day in 1955 are the following railway workers at Wickham; Alf Scarrott, Tom Hale, Frank Davies, Reg Staples, George Goddard, Ern Searle, Arthur Godwin and Freddie Boyce. The News, Portsmouth.

On the last day of passenger services 5th Feb 1955, the next Alton train is awaited as 700 Class No. 30326 waits with a down goods train at Wickham. Lens of Sutton.

Water being the only thing now waiting at Wickham station, where vegetation and undergrowth have taken over what was one of the railways longest platforms, in January 1983. R.C. Hardingham.

700 Class No. 30326 arriving at Wickham with a down goods train, on 5th Feb 1955. Lens of Sutton.

BR 4MT 2-6-4T No. 80151 prepares to do some shunting in the goods yard at Wickham. D. Fereday Glenn.

Spanning the River Meon south of Wickham, is the metal structured bridge as seen being built on page 30. In January 1983, its only use was to carry a footpath. R.C. Hardingham.

The Droxford to Fareham freight slowly approaches Knowle Junction to hand over the tablet from the Meon Valley line. U Class No. 31615 is in charge. D. Fereday Glenn.

The approach to Knowle Junction from the Meon Valley line on the 31st May 1952. Pamlin Prints, Croydon.

The now closed Knowle Halt on the Eastleigh to Fareham line. Lens of Sutton.

Class T9 4-4-0 No. 30729 restarts the down goods from Alton, at Funtley brickworks siding, on 29th Jan 1955. D. Feredey Glenn.

Knowle Junction with the Meon Valley line on the left, and the Funtley tunnel deviation line on the right, looking towards Fareham. Southern Newspapers Ltd.

Emerging from the northern portal of Funtley tunnel is C2X 0-6-0 No. 32550, with a goods train from Droxford in 1955. D. Fereday Glenn.

C2X 0-6-0 No. 32548 leaving Funtley tunnel with a Droxford to Fareham goods train in 1957. D. Fereday Glenn.

The drivers eye view coming from Fareham of Funtley tunnel entrance. The News, Portsmouth.

Funtley tunnel with Fareham station in the far distance. Author's collection.

In Coronation year on 15th June 1953, 700 Class No. 30306 is seen taking water at the Meon Valley platform at Fareham. Pamlin Prints, Croydon.

Passing Fareham signal box is an unidentified Push Pull set. Author's collection.

Fareham again on the 15th June 1953, with a U class on a Victoria train and M7 No. 30051 about to leave for Alton. Pamlin Prints, Croydon.

Just departing from Fareham 700 class No. 30689 with a Meon Valley freight. Pamlin Prints, Croydon.

Awaiting to depart from Fareham with a Sunday evening Alton train is T9 No. 30338. Author's collection.

Fareham station is dominated with the arrival of a down goods from the Meon Valley line, with T9 No. 30732. M. Gunner.

Hurrying away from Fareham with an Alton train is M7 No. 30480. Author's collection.

The modern day image of Fareham station in January 1983, looking west towards Funtley, with the closed signal box guarding the junction. R.C. Hardingham.

SERVICES - DECLINE

The Woking - Portsmouth Sunday service, first introduced in the early years, was to remain until the winter of 1951-52. Each station on the northern half of the line had cheap day facilities to Aldershot,but not to Alton and those south of Droxford, to Fareham, and in some instances to Portsmouth. These were rarely used. A cheap day return fare to London was available, but it was necessary to return on the 6.57 p.m. from Waterloo, to be able to catch the last train of the day from Alton to Fareham. In spite of this limitation,the Meon Valley route was the quickest and still was at the closure,between the Fareham area and London. One drawback, however, was undoubtedly the fact that most of the stations were situated some way out of the villages, but better publicity, coupled with more train services and cheaper fare concessions,would have done much to offset the serious loss of revenue. The more economic diesel railcars were still in their infancy and not sufficiently developed for them to be used on the Meon Valley Line.

The axe first fell in 1951. The Sunday trains were the first to go, and shortly after, the weekday passenger services were reduced to four trains in each direction, the last train down the Valley now became the 4.30 ex-Alton, which of course practically put paid to the Waterloo cheap day return, although it was still available.

Everywhere, people travelled less and less by train and as freight rates increased, even freight traffic reduced and from this time British Railways found itself with an ever growing annual deficit and was forced to resort to the "lopping off" of unremunerative branch lines, in an effort to keep down costs. The Meon Valley Line was an early candidate, parts of it being closed after a life of not much more than 50 years and it was announced that it was intended to save £39,000 a year, by withdrawing passenger services completely, and freight services from Tisted, Privett and West Meon. The date set for this was February 5th 1955, but there were objections from all sorts of people up and down the "Valley". A well attended public meeting, held at Alton, passed a resolution, expressing deep concern at the British Railways' decision to close down the passenger train service. Although freight services were to remain at either end of the line, for the time being, everyone realised that this was the thin end of the wedge and eventually trains would disappear completely.

On a well weeded track at Droxford, U Class 2-6-0 No. 31619 stands beside the up platform prior to the lines closure, in the late sixties. The signal box at this time had been demolished. M. Gunner.

In January 1955 the National Farmers Union made a strong objection to the closure and pointed out the use they made of the line during the busy sugar beet season.

This was followed by a public enquiry,

instigated by the Transport Users Committee which, of course, pronounced in favour of closure. The Chairman of the Droxford Rural District Council, was reported as saying, that the result was a foregone conclusion before the meeting started, as in fact the contract for the taking up of the track was already let by December 1954.

As with other branch lines faced with imminent closure, record sales of tickets were made during the last few weeks, staff were heard to remark that revenue of this sort would have done much to keep the line open. The announcement also brought a rush of photographers; it is thought that the Meon Valley Railway was photographed more during the last months of its life, than during its whole history.

Auto set No. 4 with M7 No. 30054 in the final months of the service. T. Wright.

By Courtesy of the Hampshire Chronicle

CLOSING THE MEON VALLEY RAILWAY

Final Public Day

On Saturday last, February 5th, the Meon Valley Railway closed, and the last public trains left Alton to travel "down" at 4.30 p.m. and Fareham to do the "up" journey at 7.46 p.m.

On the following day (Sunday) the Railway Correspondence and Travel Society organised an excursion from Waterloo, taking in not only the Meon Valley line but the Pulborough, Midhurst and Petersfield line, which had also closed the previous day. This train, with ten coaches, and drawn by two locomotives, was designated "The Hampshireman", and was crowded with railway enthusiasts. "T.J." below describes the journeys of the last public trains, and also of "The Hampshireman" through the beautiful Surrey, Sussex and Hampshire countryside, on a perfect Sunday in glorious sunshine.

THE FINAL DAY

The first man I ran into on Alton Station on Saturday, February 5th was Charlie Arthur. Charlie was making his way over the footbridge from the 3.47 p.m. arrival from Fareham, his guard's bag in his hand, his last trip on the Meon Valley completed. He said it had been a busy day. "Passengers everywhere; no time to do anything but look after passengers - not even time to read my paper." Charlie, I believe, was quite thankful his turn of duty was over.

At the platform was waiting the 4.30 p.m. for Fareham with driver Jim Elliot in charge. His train all that day consisted of four coaches instead of the usual two, his engine being Class M7 30055. At the top of her smokebox door, she carried a large rectangular green board on which was the inscription "The Last Train", and an enthusiast was in the process of attaching a holly and laurel wreath with the words:

"Vale - The Meon Valley" - February 5th 1955. Crowning the board were two Union Jacks. Photographs taken, with a long blast on the whistle, the last Alton to Fareham train pulled out promptly at 4.30 p.m.

The train was comfortably filled, and the majority of travellers were those whose practice it is to attend the last rites of dying railways. Some ladies were present and more joined at the wayside stations. Watchers in fields were given a shriek of the whistle in exchange for their waves. Farringdon - a pram unloaded; Tisted - a photographer rushed to the engine, photographed the tablet being handed over by the signalman to the driver, rushed back in the nick of time while five passengers joined and we were off down the valley to Privett. A few passengers graced the platform. As we sped along the setting sun from one window faced the rising moon from the other; dusk was falling by West Meon where more ladies joined us, possibly lured to Fareham by the reports of television which were rife - but more likely just wishing to ride in the last train.

The sun had set at Droxford - by Wickham, the moon was well up and a good dozen passengers joined the train. With much whistling we ran on to Knowle Halt where guard Barrett stepped on to the platform, looked round forlornly for passengers, found none, waved his flag and off we went through the tunnel coming to a halt in the down bay at Fareham at 5.23 p.m.

There, driver Elliot, from Fratton Shed, shook hands with the guard and a few minutes later his M7 trundled round the curve en route for her home.

The return trip was due to commence at 6.48 p.m. but the interval was far from uninteresting. The wreath was transferred with due ceremony to the engine to haul the final train. The Boards were placed in position; the flags stood aloft

M7 No. 30055 comes under the road bridge at Tisted on the last day. Lens of Sutton.

Adorned with wreath, flags and The Last Train headboard, ex-LSWR M7 No. 30055 awaits departure from Alton on the 5th February 1955 with the final scheduled Meon Valley passenger train for Fareham. R.C. Riley.

These two pictures portray the very last up passenger train from Fareham to Alton, which was hauled by Drummond 700 Class No. 30326. The right of way being given by Guard Bill Petherbridge at 6.48pm. The News, Portsmouth.

The locomotive was "700" Class 30326 with driver J.W. Dearling and fireman A.Ackehurst in charge. Typical of their class, the men enjoyed the occasion, welcomed visitors on to their footplate and posed for numerous photographs on their engine. For some rather obscure reason one of the lady passengers was induced to mount the buffer beam and be photographed with the crew.

Shortly before departure, there arrived the Chairman of Fareham U.D.C., Councillor Robert Syme, J.P. with Mrs. Syme, representatives of Wickham Parish Council, Major W.A. Tull and Mrs. Tull, and later two Droxford Parish Councillors joined the train. Rather curiously, unknown to many, was Mr. R.G. Reeves of Droxford, whose parents, it was reported, had taken the very first Meon Valley train on their honeymoon trip.

One other enthusiast disclosed that he had arrived specially from York and how that day he had made two round trips on the line. Such is the spirit of the real enthusiast. Three men joined hands, who had travelled in the first trian to run on the line, Mr. T. Clyde Britton, Alderman Keene of Fareham and Mr. Isles. Amid some laughter, they recounted their experiences on that June day over fifty years ago. Mr. A. Page, accompanied by children and grandchildren, was also present on this historic occasion.

At. 6.48 p.m. precisely, guard Barrett waved us off and amid explosions from detonators, numerous whistles and much cheering and waving, 30326 pulled her four coaches out of the bay on her twenty-three mile trip. Knowle Halt at 6.55 - little activity; Wickham at 7 p.m. presented a different picture. Crowds jostled on the platform. A number of passengers alighted as did others attracted by the unusual spectacle of so many people at the station.

All well, Station Master Squires gave the right away, the guard showed his green light but nothing happened. A minute or so later, a smiling fireman walked down the platform looking for the culprit who had pulled the communication cord. Apparently the usual financial toll was not exacted; Negotiations were brief,and the fireman walked back, mounted his engine and amid many cheers, we were off.

Droxford platform, 7.14 p.m. was graced by perhaps twenty people. There was little delay, a few well-wishers waved us goodbye and, with a long whistle, we hurried on our way. West Meon, 7.23 p.m. had produced an embryonic feminine choir which though small in number gave a fair rendering of "Auld Lang Syne" much to the amusement of passengers. A small boy was obiously being shown the last train at West Meon; perched on his father's shoulders he waved us farewell. As the last train pulled out we hoped it would not be long before he would see some more locos and satisfy that wish of all small boys.

Over the viaduct, through West Meon Tunnel, we plodded, over the Petersfield road, up to Privett Tunnel and through the cutting to the station of that name at 7.32 p.m. where another dozen or so people hailed the last train at their station. Three long whistles and they saw us disappearing under the roadbridge in a cloud of steam; rail traffic at Privett had ended. At 7.39 we reached Tisted; little delay, a few joined and off we went on the stretch of line no more to echo to the wheels of any kind of train. Farringdon Halt, 7.43 p.m., no one left. The guard, as was doubtless his wont, turned out one lamp, walked to the other,watched by many eyes, and extinguished it too. The lights were going out not only at Farringdon, but all the Meon Valley stations.

At. 7.50 p.m. we ran into Fareham line platform at Alton. Across the way was an "electric" waiting to set off for London. Here were we stepping out from our ancient carriages with their headboards "The Circus Belle" and the side of the last bearing a poster reading "To be let furnished - apply British Railways". The new and the old side by side in contrast, the swift, silent efficient, impersonal, surburban "electric" - the "Black Motor" 0-6-0, its old crimson-lake coaches, its human touch, its friendliness.

The last train arriving at Alton was once more photographed, a B.B.C. man scribbled a few notes, the enthusiasts scattered their various ways but some remained to see the headboard being removed. The wreath was laid on the platform, the flags were lowered and as the "electric" moved swiftly off – symbol of 1955 and the shape of things to come – the final obsequies were observed. The Meon Valley Railway – friendly, pleasurable, beautiful – had come to its end.

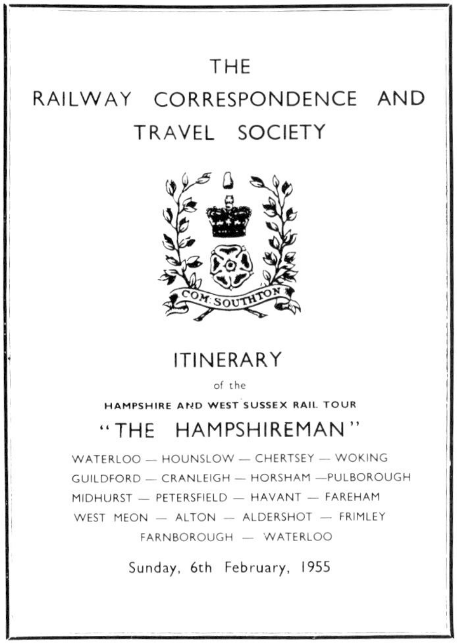

THE

RAILWAY CORRESPONDENCE AND TRAVEL SOCIETY

ITINERARY

of the

HAMPSHIRE AND WEST SUSSEX RAIL TOUR

"THE HAMPSHIREMAN"

WATERLOO — HOUNSLOW — CHERTSEY — WOKING
GUILDFORD — CRANLEIGH — HORSHAM —PULBOROUGH
MIDHURST — PETERSFIELD — HAVANT — FAREHAM
WEST MEON — ALTON — ALDERSHOT — FRIMLEY
FARNBOROUGH — WATERLOO

Sunday, 6th February, 1955

By courtesy of the R.C.T.S.

By courtesy of the Hampshire Chronicle

The Hampshireman Feb. 6th 1955

Put five or so railway enthusiasts together and watch and listen to what happens. Put five hundred or so together, sharpen their appetites with the prospect of exploration of seldom-travelled lines, promise them a spicing of unusual engines, garnish the dish with the lure of travelling over lines officially closed the previous day and their enthusiasm knows no bounds.

Five hundred and thirty rallied at Waterloo Station at 9.45 on Sunday last to join "The Hampshireman", the Railway Correspondence and Travel Society's rail tour special. Ten coaches, including a cafeteria car, were hauled by "H2" Class Atlantic 32421, bearing on her smokebox door a replica in colour of the coat of arms of Hampshire. Induced by the prospect of travelling through some wonderful railway countryside, members had arrived from as far afield as Cornwall, Ireland and Scotland.

Journey extraordinary in weather; that is the only way to describe our travels through Surrey, Sussex and Hampshire on a day when the sun shone down from a cloudless sky, when delays did not matter, when prompt arrival times were of little moment and when locomotive performance was of little account than the comfort of the compartment.

"The Hampshireman" stopped at West Meon for thirteen minutes, just enough time for photographs to be taken. Hampshire Chronicle.

We left Waterloo at 9.45 a.m. our destination being Waterloo by a circuitous itinerary of 192 miles. Woking was reached after a journey of 34 miles instead of the usual 24, but by a more interesting route. Guildford saw the "Atlantic" replaced by a couple of "E5X" Class engines, 32570 and 32576. Destination was now Petersfield via Horsham. By lovely wooded Sussex scenery, we wended our way; and by the line closed officially the previous day to passenger traffic we reached Midhurst. After a short stop for photographs at that historic railway town, we ambled along a line, now completely closed by the way of Elsted and Rogate stations, greeted all the way by enthusiastic spectators.

We Crossed the Hampshire border near Petersfield where a number of scholars from Churchers College lined up to watch us approach the main line; one or two mounted a ganger's hut and sounded "The Last Post" as we crawled past.

Petersfield saw another change of engines. We were now headed by two of the "T9" Class, 30732 and 30301. Off once more, climbing the three miles to the summit at Buriton Tunnel, the bark of the engines' exhausts and their sharp whistles echoing in the deep chalk cuttings. South of the tunnel and gathering speed, we twisted and turned on the reverse curves, the sweep of the Downs at first close at hand and then gradually becoming more distant as we galloped through Rowlands Castle and braked sharply to round the curve into Havant. Along the coast to Fareham and on we went to the Meon Valley railway proper; past Knowle Halt where some witty exchanges were made with the signalman, past Wickham, through Droxford, both with people on the platforms, cheering us on our way and so to West Meon at 3.30 p.m.

The good folk of West Meon, on a peaceful, sunny, Sunday afternoon, have never witnessed before such a spectacle - nor are they ever likely in the future to enjoy a repetition. We were booked to stop for 15 minutes to allow photographs to be taken. The moment the train halted, every door opened - whether on the platform side or not - and hundreds took advantage of the opportunity presented. Scores climbed the sides of the deep cuttings, many mounted the roadbridge parapets and all sought vantage points which would lend themselves to the taking of a picture of the railway scene;-one enterprising youth set a fine pace by climbing the home signal. While the engines took water, the R.C.T.S. took possession of West Meon station; shutters clicked, a B.B.C. man made some recordings and the booking office did a roaring trade in selling single tickets to Privett and Droxford. Incredible conduct it must have seemed to the people on the platform.

Despite several appealing blasts on the whistle to make the travellers return to their coaches, no heed was taken until the drivers decided, willy-nilly, to start. Thereupon a

Large plumes of smoke against the evening sky, as T9s Nos. 30301 and 30732 hurry Northwards towards Alton, paying a final farewell to the Meon Valley Railway. E.C. Griffith.

frantic rush was made for the doors. No one was left though there were several "near misses". Amid the cheers of the bewildered West Meonites, the last and longest passenger train drew out of the station and peace descende once more on that quiet Hampshire village.

Privett, grass grown and deserted, was graced by one or two people, but no time was spent there. With a whistle-salute, we were under the road-bridge and on our way to Tisted. Most of the way, cars were lined up by the roadside and watchers, on roads, in fields, in wayside cottages, on farms and on the embankments themselves, waved as we passed. Gently we slackened speed to exchange the tablet - the last tablet, the last station, the last train - and many hands were waved in response to the cheering crowd lining the platform.

One has a feeling of taking part in a historic drama on leaving a station destined no more to hear the passing of trains. It is strange to reflect that, a mere fifty years ago, the people of these villages were welcoming the new means of transport with delight and that now their trains have gone, for good, never to return. We were writing a page in history as we drew out of Tisted on Sunday.

We swept on gathering speed. Farringdon Halt - a few spectators - and on to Butts Junction and Alton where the Meon Valley Line ends. From there on "electric" tracks, one crossed the Hampshire border near Bentley en route for Waterloo.

"An unforgettable day, in glorious sunshine, an excellent tour over a most interesting route"; that was the R.C.T.S. paid tribute to the Midhurst line and the Meon Valley Railway, and how they erected a memorial to these well-loved branches. The visit of The Hampshireman will long be remembered by the countless spectators who watched and cheered his passing. And how these railway enthusiasts can enjoy themselves. Some day, I think I may even become one myself.

DEMOLITION BEGINS

It seems ironic that after spending several years gathering photographs and information on the Meon Valley Railway and eventually putting it together to form a book which in effect was written to perpetuate the memory of the line, I was one of the many people who helped to dismantle it and send the scrap away for repro-cessing. In 1955, at the time of the withdrawal of the passenger service and the closure of the

R.C.T.S. Special 'The Hampshireman' at Alton, with T9s Nos. 30301 and 30732 at the head, after arrival from Fareham on 6th Feb 1955. The day before, passenger services were withdrawn over the whole of the Meon Valley line. T. Wright.

middle section of the line (i.e. Tisted, Privett and West Meon), my grandfather, William Stone of the New Inn, West Meon, was running the family coal and haulage business and I was employed by him as a driver.

British Railways, had by this time, removed everything needed by them for re-use, such as office furniture, platform barrows, fire buckets, scales, paraffin cans etc., while barrow loads of tickets were burnt in the goods yards. Towards the end of 1955 we learned that Messrs Thomas Ward of London had obtained the contract to remove the rails, sleepers, signals and telephone lines, in fact all scrap metal, which included the West Meon Viaduct. It was at this time that they approached William Stone to see if they might hire a lorry and driver for a year or so to assist in the dismantling. This was agreed to and we were requested to report one Monday morning to Privett station, where the headquarters of the operations, including early morning tea, were based in the signal box.

First to go were the telephone wires, taken down and rolled into bundles before being taken to Farringdon to be put into box wagons for dispatch to London. Then began the lifting of the track at Tisted. The rails were levered out of the chairs and loaded onto timber lorries. The steel sleers were cut in half and the timber ones in the goods yard were mostly purchased by my grandfather for re-sale.

Worst of all was the work in Privett tunnel, 1056 yards in length and shaped like an 'S' meant that to be anywhere near the middle of the tunnel, with no lights, one was in a darkness so deep as to defy description.

Slowly but surely, piece by piece, the Meon Valley Railway began to disappear. Several people purchased the station lamps, complete with standards, to stand outside their homes. Former railway employees were given the opportunity to buy such things as the windows from the signal boxes, whilst the paraffin shed at West Meon still stands at the railway cottages as a garden shed.

South of West Meon station, from Hayden Lane to Meonstoke, the track had been laid on concrete sleepers and these were lifted and taken by William Stone lorries down to the River Hamble to be made into a jetty.

The year 1956 saw the beginning of the removal of the grandest sight of all - the West Meon Viaduct and of course it was photographed more during this time than during the whole life of the railway. After removal of the track, the ballast was moved simply by cutting a hole in the floor and then by shovelling the whole lot through,

Demolition is underway on the viaduct in 1956, this being one of the first parts of the railway to be dismantled due to its high scrap value. The men in the photograph are shovelling ballast through a gap in the structure. P. Snow.

for it to fall on the bank beneath. The photographs will show that the centre pier was felled like a tree, to fall on the southern embankment to be cut up into more manageable sections. Many people were saddened to see the viaduct go, indeed my grandfather, William Stone, reflected that he and his mother had served breakfast at the New Inn, West Meon to the night shift navvies who were engaged in its construction. But maybe it was not to last much longer anyway as it was found that rust had eaten into the structure up to 2½ inches in places.

Standing like statues, the remaining pillars dwarf a local Southdown bus passing through West Meon village. Author's collection.

Going, Going.

Gone!   *Both W.S. Poole*

REMAINING SERVICES

Following the closure, the commencement of a daily Portsmouth to Alton bus service introduced by the Southdown Bus Company, was to serve the places which had lost its rail service. Ironically though, a strike caused the service to be cancelled for a while at the start. Good use was made of the service with many children going to school in Alton by luxury buses.

The Meon Valley still had some trains running though, with a daily goods service running over the two severed sections. At the Alton end a goods train ran as far as Farringdon before shunting and reversing to Alton. Similarly a goods train ran from Fareham to serve Wickham, Mislingford and finally to Droxford to return tender first to Fareham. Surprisingly, this service was to last longer than most people expected, but after a year or so it was reduced to just three days a week. The Droxford goods service finally gave up the ghost on 30th April 1962, with the Farringdon goods lingering on until 13th August 1968, when BR announced that the last operational fragment of the Meon Valley line was to close.

Taking water is U Class No. 31809 at Alton station, with the Farringdon goods train on 3rd July 1965. Ken Cole.

After arrival from Alton, No. 31809 is seen shunting its train of BOCM vans at Farringdon on 3rd July 1965. Ken Cole.

Farringdon sidings on 3rd July 1965 and U Class No. 31809 waits to return to Alton. Ken Cole.

On its return from Farringdon, No. 31809 waits in the up yard at Alton, to work the 10.32am freight to Feltham, as a 2-BIL with the 07.55 from Waterloo nears the station, on 3rd July 1965. Ken Cole.

THE PRESERVATION ERA

The remaining southern section from Knowle to Droxford was to see continued activity following closure by BR. Mr. Charles Ashby was to take over Droxford station to test his ingenious 'Pacerailer' railbus. This vehicle was put to test on a special 1 in 10 incline section, built especially for it, in an attempt to convince prospective purchasers of its capabilities. (It is interesting to note now that BR have subsequently designed a very similar vehicle). For a short while, A1X No. 32646 was to be seen at Droxford, but was to leave in May 1966 for Hayling Island to stand outside a public house. In 1965 some preservationists in the form of the Southern Locomotive Preservation Company approached Mr. Ashby with a view to having their stock at Droxford too, no doubt with the long term possible opening of the remaining section in mind. The SLP gradually moved in their items of stock which included several wagons and ex-Southall Gas Works Ruston Hornsby 88DS diesel shunter named 'Spitfire'. But the largest locomotive to arrive was USA 0-6-0T No. 30064 in January 1969, rescued from Salisbury motive power depot along with No. 30072 which was to go to the Keighley & Worth Valley Railway. No sooner had No. 30064 arrived than the SLP began to see that the future at Droxford was looking uncertain. Several trips were made down the line using No. 30064 and Maunsell coach No. 6686, but problems were being encountered with vandals breaking into Mr. Ashby's 'Pacerailer', indeed causing considerable damage. The proposal to form a preservation centre on the Longmoor Military Railway at Liss was also gaining momentum with backing being received from some important railway preservation bodies. Thus any scheme to run trains on what was left of the Meon Valley Railway would receive less support or attention. Finally, BR decided to close Knowle junction and this was to be the final straw for the SLP.

Prior to being offered for sale, A1X 0-6-0 No. 32646 stands in a desolate Droxford station. The loco was sold eventually to Brickwoods for one of their Hayling Island public houses, where it stood outside for several years, before finally returning to its original work place on the Isle of Wight. Author's collection.

This diesel shunter, Ruston Hornsby No. 200793, came to Droxford from Kilmersdon Colliery in July 1967. J.R. Fairman.

An assortment of items at Droxford. J.R. Fairman.

Sadler "Pacerailer" railbus at Droxford on 28th Jan 1967. S.C. Nash.

Looking lost against a platform length of 600ft either side, built for ten coach Waterloo to Gosport trains, ex Southall Gas works diesel shunter named "Spitfire" stands silent with a private special to Droxford at Wickham, on 28th Jan 1967. S.C. Nash.

They decided to remove all their stock firstly to Fareham and then to Liss only to find out, a year later, that the scheme there was also to fail. A home was fortunately provided by The Bluebell Railway in Sussex where ten years' service has been accomplished by No. 30064 and other items of rolling stock to the enjoyment of many.

CHOCOLATE COMMERCIAL

The short section of railway between the Butts and Farringdon was used in September 1968 to make a television commercial for Cadburys Milk Tray. A train supplied by BR made up of a diesel locomotive and two coaches made several trips during the filming. This section of track was then lifted during the period November 1969 and May 1970.

FARMERS TAKE OVER

The track bed, or what remained of it, was put to various uses. At the northern end, close to the Butts, some bridges have been dismantled to make way for the Alton by-pass and from there to Hedge Corner adjoining land-owners have purchased the land, filling in cuttings and removing embankments, so that in places the countryside has been restored to its pre-1900 state.

The section between West Meon station and Knowle was purchased by the Hampshire County Council and was designated a nature walk, with the old goods yard serving as a depot for road making materials. West Meon tunnel has been used by a company breaking up aircraft fuselages, whilst the tunnel at Privett was, for some time, used for growing mushrooms!

Considering the short life of the Meon Valley Railway (a little over 50 years) it seems difficult to justify the tremendous effort put in by the navvies and the loss of life, to construct what in all amounted to a mere 22½ miles of new railway.

With the passing of the railway and similar lines, we have seen a way of life disappear forever. We can now only gaze with nostalgia at the overgrown platforms and ivy covered bridges.

Mr. C. Ashby left, and Mr. Ray Stone, author, travel on the last remaining section of the Meon Valley line between Wickham and Droxford in April 1973. This was probably the last occasion that a railed vehicle travelled on the Meon Valley Railway. E.C. Griffith.

Appendix 1

LONDON AND SOUTH WESTERN RAILWAY
TIME TABLE – 7th June to 30th September 1914

WEEKDAYS DOWN

	AM	AM	AM	PM	PM	PM	PM
ALTON Dep.	8.57	11.12	11.55	3.09	5.46	7.06	
TISTED Arr.	9.07	11.22	12.05	3.19	5.56	7.16	
PRIVETT Arr.	9.14	11.32	12.12	3.26	6.03	7.23	
WEST MEON Arr.	9.21	11.39	12.19	3.33	6.10	7.31	10.30
DROXFORD Arr.	9.29	11.46	12.26	3.40	6.17	7.39	10.36
WICKHAM Arr.	9.37	11.57	12.34	3.48	6.25	7.47	10.44
KNOWLE Platform	9.43	–	12.39	N	–	P	–
FAREHAM Arr.	9.48	12.06	12.44	3.57	6.34	7.56	10.53

NOTES N Stops at Knowle Platform on Thursdays to take up or set down passengers.

P Stops at Knowle Platform on Saturdays to take up or set down passengers.

SUNDAYS DOWN

ALTON Dep.	–	10.50	8.20	
TISTED Arr.	–	10.59	8.29	(Tisted for Selborne)
PRIVETT Arr.	–	11.06	8.36	
WEST MEON Arr.	–	11.13	8.43	
DROXFORD Arr.	–	11.20	8.50	(Droxford for Hambledon)
WICKHAM Arr.	8.40	11.28	8.58	
KNOWLE Platform	–	–	–	
FAREHAM Arr.	8.48	11.37	9.07	

WEEKDAYS UP

	AM	AM	PM	PM	PM	PM	PM
FAREHAM Dep.	7.30	10.41	1.37	4.30	5.55	7.35	9.52
KNOWLE Platform	–	10.46	RQ	–	–	7.40	9.57
WICKHAM	7.39	10.51	1.46	4.39	6.04	7.49	10.02
DROXFORD	7.50	11.01	1.56	4.49	6.19	8.00	10.12
WEST MEON	7.59	11.09	2.04	4.58	6.27	8.08	10.19
PRIVETT	8.09	11.19	2.14	5.08	6.37	8.18	
TISTED	8.15	11.25	2.20	5.14	6.43	8.24	
ALTON Arr.	8.23	11.33	2.28	5.22	6.51	8.32	

NOTES

Q Stops at Knowle Platform on the last Wednesday in each month to take up or set down passengers.

R Stops at Knowle Platform on Thursdays to take up or set down passengers.

SUNDAYS UP

FAREHAM Dep.	7.48	8.30	7.20
KNOWLE Platform	–	–	7.26
WICKHAM	7.56	8.39	7.32
DROXFORD		8.49	7.44
WEST MEON		8.57	7.54
PRIVETT		9.07	8.05
TISTED		9.13	8.12
ALTON Arr.		9.21	8.20

BRITISH RAILWAYS (Southern Region) TIME TABLE

From 20th September 1954

WEEKDAYS UP

	AM	AM	PM	PM
FAREHAM Dep.	7.58	11.56	2.48	6.48
KNOWLE Platform	8.02	12.00	2.53	6.53
WICKHAM	8.07	12.05	2.58	6.58
DROXFORD (B)	8.17	12.15	3.08	7.08
WEST MEON	8.25	12.23	3.18	7.17
PRIVETT	8.34	12.32	3.29	7.27
TISTED (A)	8.40	12.38	3.36	7.34
FARRINGDON	8.44	12.42	3.40	7.38
ALTON Arr.	8.51	12.49	3.47	7.46

NOTES A. Station for Selborne 4½ miles.
B. Station for Hambledon 3½ miles.

SUNDAYS NO SERVICE

WEEKDAYS DOWN

	AM	AM	PM	PM
ALTON Dep.	7.38	9.05	1.30	4.30
FARRINGDON	7.45	9.12	1.37	4.37
TISTED	7.50	9.16	1.41	4.41
PRIVETT	7.57	9.24	1.49	4.48
WEST MEON	8.05	9.31	1.56	4.56
DROXFORD (B)	8.15	9.39	2.04	5.03
WICKHAM	8.27	9.48	2.12	5.12
KNOWLE HALT	8.32	9.54	2.18	5.18
FAREHAM Arr.	8.37	9.59	2.23	5.23

Appendix 2

The Board of Trade Inspecting Officer's report on the works of the Meon Valley Railway.

RAILWAY DEPARTMENT,

...CEIVED 6 - APR ...3
...o. 4081

BOARD OF TRADE,

8, *Richmond Terrace,*

Whitehall, London, S.W.

SIR,

I have the honour to report for the information of the Board of Trade, that in compliance with the instructions contained in your Minute of the 16th March, I made an inspection on the 2nd and 3rd Instants of the new works on the Meon Valley Railway constructed by the L & S. W. Railway Company.

Of the two railways authorised by the Company's Act, Railway No. 2 has alone been completed.

This line commences by a junction with the Company's Farnham, Alton, and Winchester branch, at Butts Junction, and has a general S.S.W. direction terminating by a junction with the Company's Bishopstoke & Portsmouth Line near Fareham Station.

The total length of Ry. No. 2 is ~~&~~ 22 miles 24. 25 chs.

The authorised limits of lateral & horizontal deviation do not appear to have been exceeded. The line is single throughout except at stations, where loops are provided. The gauge is 4' 8½".

Land has been purchased for a double line, and double line over bridges have been built, but some of the underbridges have only been constructed for a single line of way.

The ruling gradient has an inclination of 1 in 90, with a length of 47 chs, The sharpest curve (except at junctions where 20 chs curves exist) has a radius of 37 chs. & a length of 33 chs.

Formation — the width for a single line is 19 ft. The space between double lines is 6 ft. Between the main line & sidings there is (~~there~~ except at Tisted Stⁿ.) a space of not less than 9½ ft. Between the sides of the widest carriage & any fixed work there is a minimum clearance of 2' 4".

Fencing — three types are used

I. Post with 4 horizontal rails — 4' high

2. Post with diagonal rails — 4½' high

3. Galvanized wire, — 8 wires — 4¼' high

<u>Drainage</u> – the usual ditches on the higher sides of cuttings & banks have been provided.

<u>Permanent Way</u> – bullheaded rails in 30' lengths, weighing 87 lbs per yd, are laid on C.I. chairs weighing 47 lbs each. The chairs are fastened to ~~the~~ ordinary creosoted sleepers by 3 trenails & 5/8" spikes. The sleepers are spaced at 2½' average central intervals. The Rails are jointed by bracketed fishplates, weighing 40 lbs per pair. The ballast consists partly of Southampton gravel, & partly of local gravel. The permanent way is in a satisfactory condition, & the line is well ballasted throughout.

<u>Earthwork</u> – for the first 17 miles, the cuttings are carried through chalk with gravel top soil, thence to the termination through clay & sand. The heaviest work is to be found between miles 7¾ & 11¼, where there is a length of 20 chs of cutting with a max. depth of 70'. There is a second length of about 60 chs with a max. depth of 69'. The largest Embankment has a length of 59 chs with a max. height of 62'. Slips have occurred about mile 18 in ~~a~~ clay cuttings, ~~and~~ & a retaining wall has been built along the toe of the slope. The movement appears to have been checked. Some of the banks were completed nine months ago, & will require careful maintenance.

Tunnels – there are two of these:–
1. at mile 7. ch. 73. length 1056 yds. constructed for a double line of way; portions of the lining are built in brick in lime mortar, & portions in cement concrete. Recesses have been provided on alternate sides at 25 yds interval. There is no special provision for ventilation; the thickness of brick lining is from 1'6" to 1'10½".
2. at mile 10, ch. 32. length 539 yds. construction is similar at No. 1. Both these tunnels are carried through chalk, have dry interiors, & show no signs of weakness.

Bridging. There are 21 overbridges, three having girder, and the remainder arched spans. In each case there is a single span varying in length from 28 feet to 50 feet. There are 43 underbridges, twenty of which have wrought iron girder or steel troughing spans, and the remainder arched spans. All of the latter has a single span from 9' to 50 feet in length. Of the metal underbridges, one over the River Meon at mile 20-46 has three spans of 27' and 28', and the others have each a single span of from 7' to 51¾' measured on the skew. The abutments and arching in all these bridges is constructed of red brickwork, in some instances faced with blue brickwork; the masonry work has a solid appearance & shows no signs of weakness.

Viaducts. There is one of these near West Meon Station at mile 11-17. The length is 77 yards, and it consists of four plate girder spans from 51 to 58 feet in length. The maximum height is 63½ feet. ~~The~~ Steel piers on concrete foundations are used. Solid concrete piers were first proposed, but some weakness in foundations was indicated, and the present type of construction was consequently adopted. I could detect no indication of movement in the concrete footings.

I tested all the wrought ironwork and steel troughing in the viaduct & under bridges, and found moderate deflections ~~[illegible]~~ from the engine load, and sufficient theoretical strength has been provided.

Culverts. There are 7 of these with spans of from 4' to 10'.

Level crossings - There are 19 level crossings, four of public and 6 of private footpaths, and 9 of occupation roads.

Sidings & Stations, Signalling etc

Butts Junction. The arrangements at this termination of the new railway were reported upon after my inspection in May 1901. The only alterations effected have been the removal of a ground disc signal, & certain interlocking.

The frame in the signal cabin contains 40 levers of which 5 will be spare when the new line is opened, and 1 is a "push & pull" lever. The Company at present have 3 down distant signals referring to the three single lines, which ~~have~~ junction here. They wish permission to remove two of these distant signals, leaving one only in use. As all down trains have to slow to pick up the train tablet, I see no objection to this proposal, which will result in making two more levers spare. The single distant signal could be lead by either one of the three sets of stop signals in front.

Farringdon Siding - at about mile 2½. There is a single set of facing points leading to sidings. The points are worked from a ground frame containing 4 levers, & is opened by the train tablet for the section.

Tisted Station - there is a loopline here for passing trains, and two platforms. On one platform there is a shelter for passengers, and on the other a booking hall, ladies room & conveniences for both sexes. The platforms are 200 yds long & 3 feet high & are connected by means of a footbridge.

On account of the rising gradient 1/100, it will be necessary to place all down trains in sidings clear of the main line before shunting operations are commenced, and a siding ~~on the down~~ long enough to contain the longest trains has been provided for the purpose.

The frame in the signal cabin contains 23 levers of which 5 are spare.

Privett Station - at 7 miles 34 chns - The arrangements at this station are similar as regards accommodation etc as at Tisted. All up trains will in this case have to be placed in sidings before shunting is commenced, and a siding for the purpose has been provided.

The frame in the signal cabin contains 25 levers of which 6 are spare.

West Meon Station - at 11 miles 42 chns - Similar arrangements & accommodation as for the last named stations.

The frame in the signal cabin contains 25 levers of which 6 are spare.

At this place the parish clerk presented me with a petition

from the parish council, which I attach (Enclosure A)
I inspected the spot where danger was anticipated, and in my opinion the danger has always been in existence owing to a sharp turn in the public road. I do not think there are grounds therefore for any action by the Board of Trade.

Droxford Station – at 15 miles 29 chns – accommodation is provided as at other stations. Up trains in view of the rising gradient must be placed in sidings before shunting is commenced, & provision for this has been made.

The frame contains 24 levers of which 5 are spare.

Mislingford Siding at 18 miles 40 chns – A single connection leading to sidings, which is worked from a ground frame containing 4 levers, opened by the train tablet for the section. In this case if up trains using this siding cannot be contained within the limits of the flat gradient of 1/330, the train must be placed within the siding points before shunting operations are commenced.

Wickham Station – at 20 miles 39 chns – Similar accommodation as at other stations –

It will be necessary here to place down trains in the siding provided for the purpose, before shunting operations are commenced –

The frame contains 24 levers, of which 6 are spare.

Knowle Junction – the Southern termination of the new ; ~~[illegible]~~ the Single line terminates with a double junction with the Portsmouth main road, between Fareham & Botley Stations.

The signal cabin is new, & will replace ~~[illegible]~~ a former block post known ~~[illegible]~~ as Knowle Siding, from which an old

siding connection is at present worked. This old connection will, after the opening of the new line, be worked from a ground frame containing 5 levers all in use, which is bolt locked from Knowle Junction Signal cabin. A new crossover road has also (new) been provided.
The frame in the signal cabin contains 25 levers of which 6 are spare.

The interlocking at all these ground frames & signal cabins is correct.

A | It will be necessary to fix lamps, and clocks at all the stations, before opening the new line for traffic, and the connections with signals & points will have to made, and existing trap points removed, also a temporary watering arrangement at Wickham.

The new railway is equipped for single line working by the Electric tablet system, & I found the necessary tablet instruments installed at Butts Junction, Tisted, Privett, West Meon, Droxford & Wickham Stations, and at Knowle Junction. The Company should submit the necessary undertaking as regards this method of working.

Subject to the receipt of this undertaking, & to the proper completion of the works referred to at A, I can advise the Board of Trade to authorize this new railway for passenger traffic.

I have etc

J. W. Pringle

Appendix 3

London & South Western Railway.

Secretary's Office,

Waterloo Station,

London, 18th May, 1903.

RECEIVED 19 MAY 1903
No. 576
BOARD OF TRADE

Sir,

I beg to enclose a plan and signal diagram shewing the alterations which have been made in the running roads in connection with improvements at Alton Station, and shall be glad to have permission to bring the same into use on the understanding that any requirements of the Inspecting Officer will be duly complied with.

The works will be ready for inspection on or after Monday the 25th instant, and we are anxious to have the benefit of the improved accommodation in connection with the opening of the Meon Valley new Line.

I am, Sir,

Your obediant Servant,

G. Knight

Secretary.

The Assistant Secretary,

Railway Department, Board of Trade.

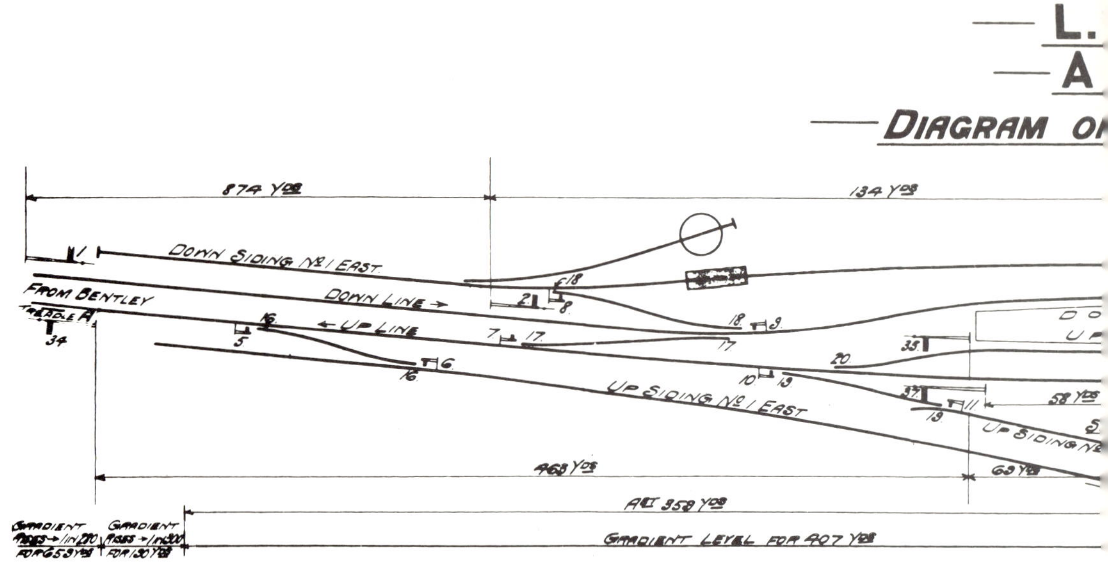
L.
A
DIAGRAM O
874 YDS
134 YDS
DOWN SIDING NO 1 EAST
DOWN LINE →
FROM BENTLEY
TREADLE A
← UP LINE
UP SIDING NO 1 EAST
468 YDS
63 YDS
58 YDS
ABT 358 YDS
GRADIENT RISES → 1 IN 270 FOR 653 YDS
GRADIENT RISES → 1 IN 300 FOR 130 YDS
GRADIENT LEVEL FOR 407 YDS

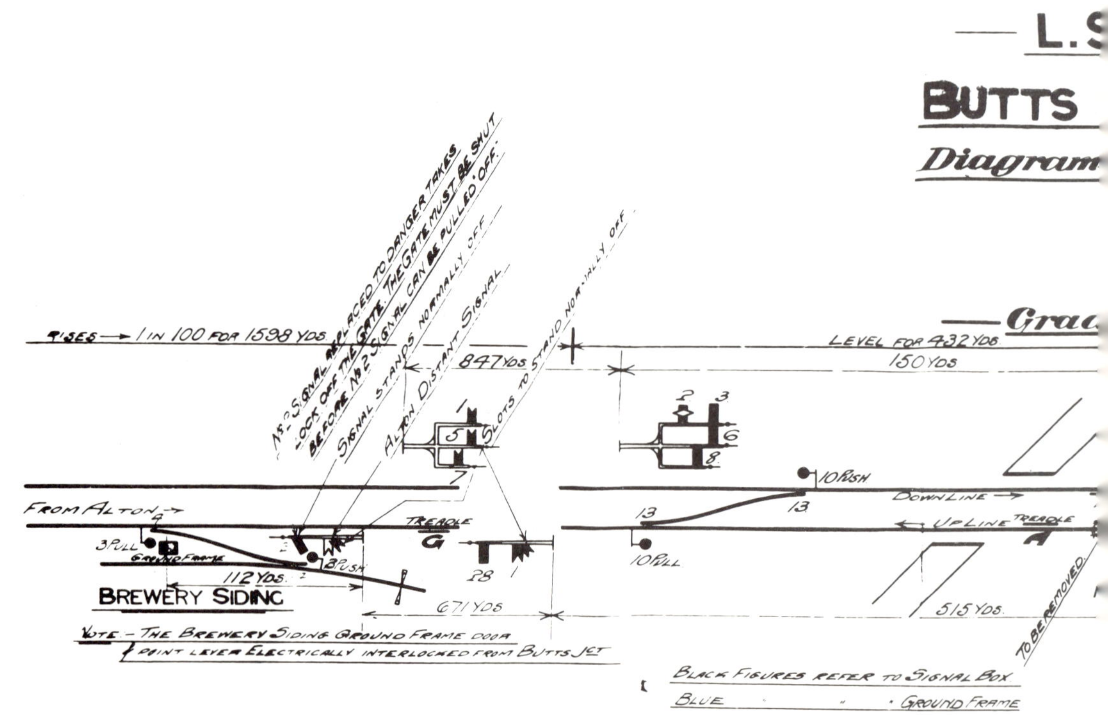
L.S
BUTTS
Diagram
Grad
RISES → 1 IN 100 FOR 1598 YDS
LEVEL FOR 432 YDS
847 YDS
150 YDS
NO 2 SIGNAL REPLACED TO DANGER TAKES LOCK OFF THE GATE. THE GATE MUST BE SHUT BEFORE NO 2 SIGNAL CAN BE PULLED 'OFF'.
SIGNAL STANDS NORMALLY OFF
ALTON DISTANT SIGNAL
SLOTS TO STAND NORMALLY OFF
FROM ALTON →
TREADLE G
3 PULL
GROUND FRAME
3 PUSH
112 YDS.
BREWERY SIDING
671 YDS
10 PUSH
DOWN LINE →
← UP LINE
TREADLE A
10 PULL
515 YDS.
TO BE REMOVED
NOTE – THE BREWERY SIDING GROUND FRAME DOOR & POINT LEVER ELECTRICALLY INTERLOCKED FROM BUTTS JCT
BLACK FIGURES REFER TO SIGNAL BOX
BLUE " " GROUND FRAME

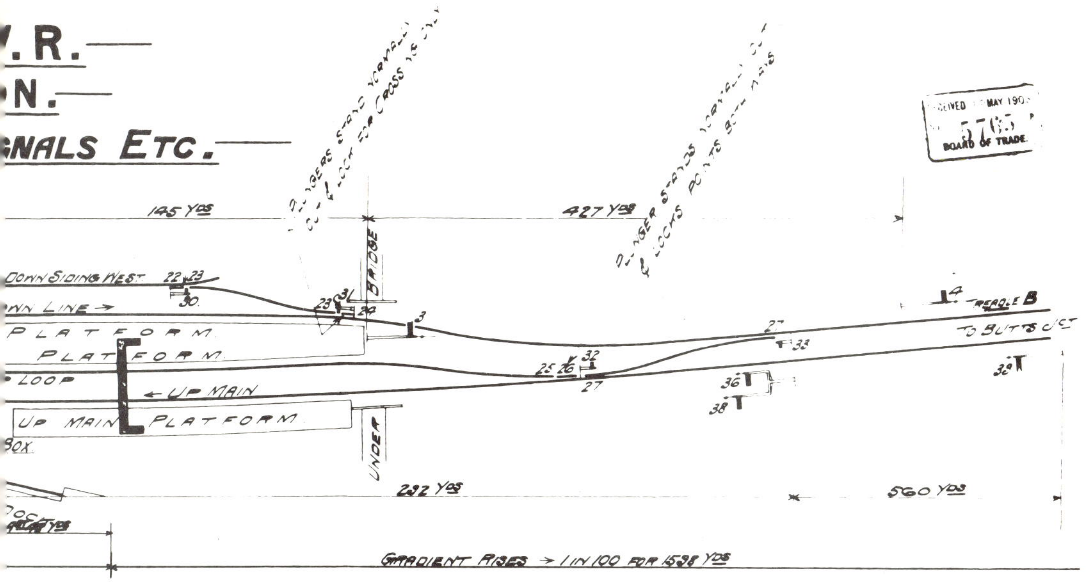
.R.
N.
NALS ETC.
145 YDS
427 YDS
DOWN SIDING WEST
DOWN LINE →
PLATFORM
PLATFORM
LOOP
← UP MAIN
UP MAIN PLATFORM
BOX
BRIDGE
UNDER
TREADLE B
TO BUTTS JCT
232 YDS
560 YDS
GRADIENT RISES → 1 IN 100 FOR 1538 YDS
RECEIVED MAY 1905
BOARD OF TRADE

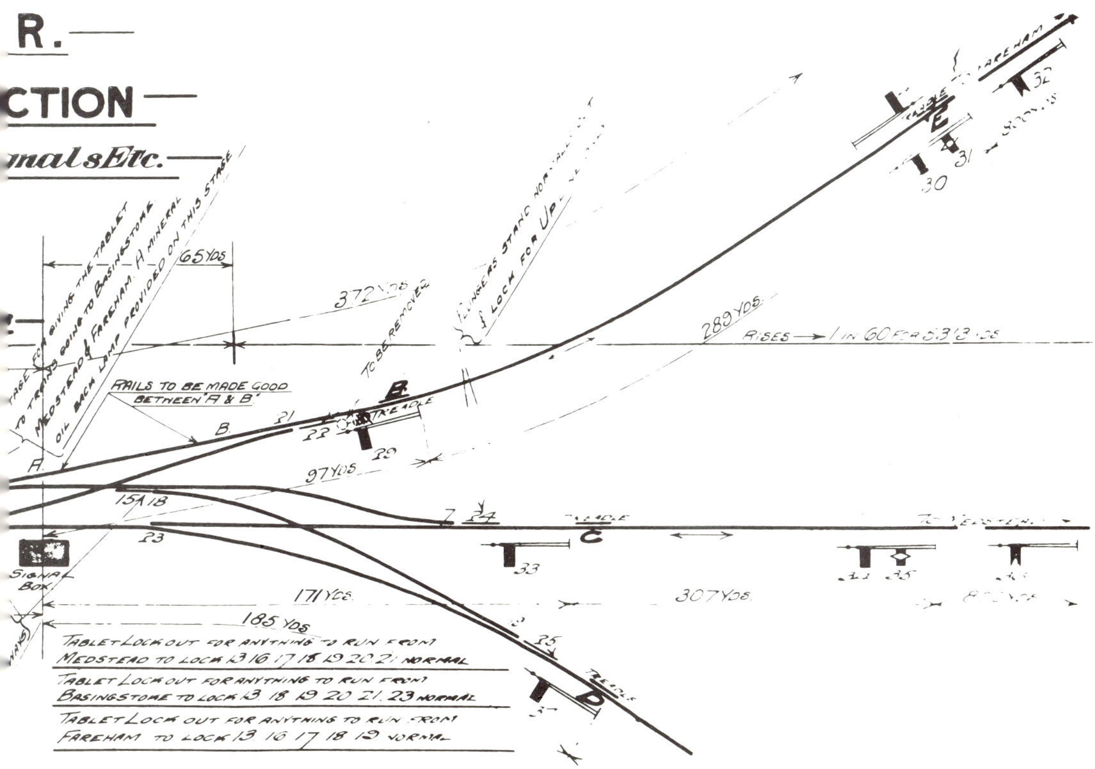
R.
CTION
nalsEtc.
65 YDS
372 YDS
289 YDS
RISES → 1 IN 60 FOR
TO BE REMOVED
RAILS TO BE MADE GOOD BETWEEN 'A' & 'B'
97 YDS
SIGNAL BOX
171 YDS
307 YDS
185 YDS
TABLET LOCK OUT FOR ANYTHING TO RUN FROM MEDSTEAD TO LOCK 13 16 17 18 19 20 21 NORMAL
TABLET LOCK OUT FOR ANYTHING TO RUN FROM BASINGSTOKE TO LOCK 13 18 19 20 21 23 NORMAL
TABLET LOCK OUT FOR ANYTHING TO RUN FROM FAREHAM TO LOCK 13 16 17 18 19 NORMAL

The Board of Trade Inspecting Officer's report on the alterations at Alton.

RAILWAY DEPARTMENT,

BOARD OF TRADE,

8, *Richmond Terrace,*

Whitehall, London, S.W.

27 June 1903

RECEIVED JUN 1903 7634 R. OF TRADE

SIR,

I have the honour to report for the information of the Board of Trade, that in compliance with the instructions contained in your Minute of the 19th May, I made an inspection today of the new works at Alton Station on the London & S.W. Railway.

The works consist of the following additions & alterations:—

A new line for down passenger traffic has been laid through the station: the old down line has been converted into an up loop line: the old down platform has been turned into an island platform: there are two new crossovers one at either end of the station, and the new signalling & working arrangements are worked from a new signal cabin. There is one set of facing points provided with the necessary safety appliances.

In connection with the new passenger road, a new span has been added to the road underbridge at the west end of the station. This has a clear span of 30 feet & the railway line is carried on W.I. plate girders with pressed steel flooring:

I tested this bridge under engine load & found that the iron & steel work gave moderate deflections. Sufficient theoretical strength has been provided.

The permanent way of the new passenger line consists of the Company's latest type of 90 lb steel rails; I have described this type in several of my recent reports on new widenings. The road is in a satisfactory condition.

The station buildings on the old down platform are now being remodelled, but the work was not in a finished condition.

The new signal cabin contains a frame with 39 levers of which 7 are spare.

I have the following requirements to make:—

a) No. 22 lever to release No. 3 when 23 is pulled.

b) An indicator repeater ~~from~~ for No. 30 ground disc signal to be provided in the signal cabin

In view of the rising gradient between the down starting & advance starting signals, I do not consider that goods trains should be held at the advance starting signal, & the Company agreed to give the necessary instructions.

Subject therefore to the completion of the named requirements I can advise the Board of Trade to sanction these new works.

The Company promised to forward a detailed plan of the new bridge referred to, a drawing of which has not yet been received by the Board.

Appendix 4

JUNE 1912

CHEAP WEEK-END TICKETS EVERY FRIDAY, SATURDAY AND SUNDAY

From:- Waterloo, Vauxhall, Queens Road, Hammersmith, Shepherds Bush, Kensington, West Brompton, Chelsea and Fulham, Battersea, Clapham Junction and Wimbledon.

TO	1st Class	2nd Class	3rd Class	
ALTON	10s 6d	6s 9d	5s 3d	
TISTED	11s 9d	7s 6d	6s 0d	
PRIVETT	12s 3d	7s 9d	6s 3d	
WEST MEON	13s 3d	8s 3d	6s 9d	
DROXFORD	14s 0d	8s 9d	7s 0d	Tickets
WICKHAM	15s 3d	9s 6d	7s 9d	issued to
FAREHAM (via Eastleigh or West Meon)	16s 6d	10s 6d	8s 3d	Bursledon via
MEDSTEAD	11s 6d	7s 3d	5s 9d	West Meon on
BENTWORTH & LASHAM				Sundays when
(via Alton)	11s 6d	7s 6d	5s 9d	Service
BURSLEDON (via West Meon)	17s 9d	11s 0d	9s 0d	permits

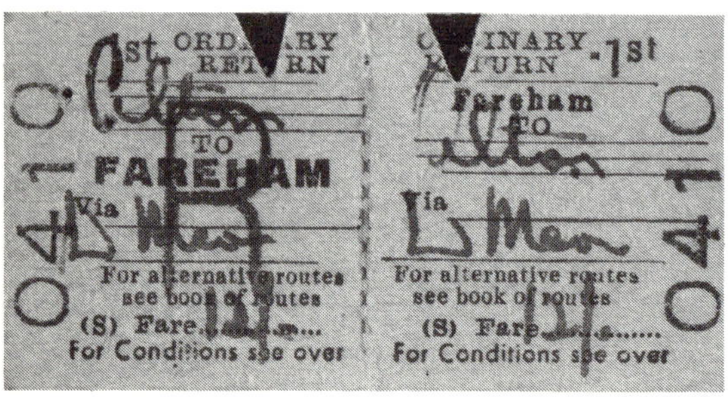

Above; Some luggage labels that still survive.
Left; A ticket issued on the last day.

Appendix 5

FARRINGDON SIDING

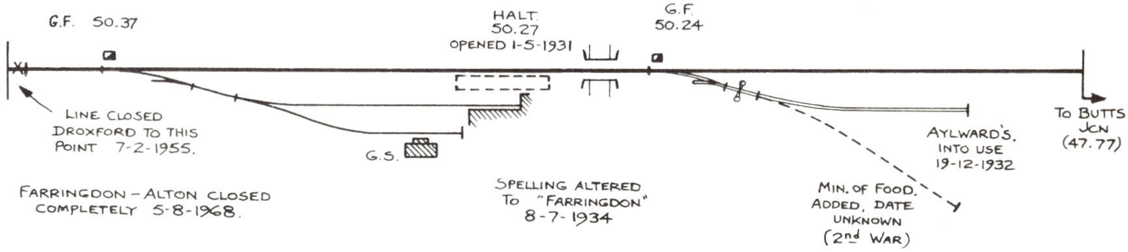

TISTED

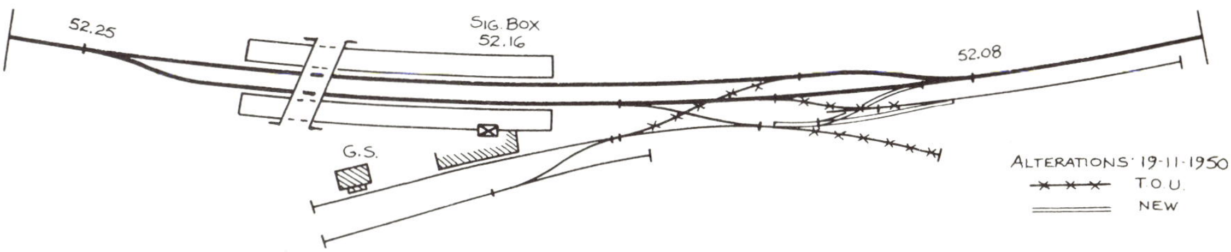

PRIVETT

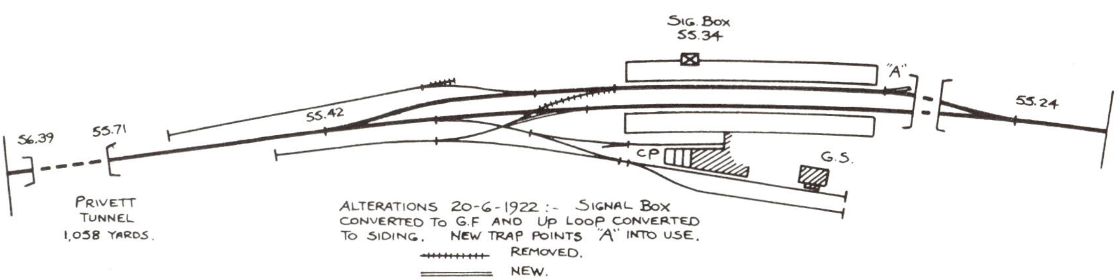

Track plans by courtesy of G.A. Pryer and A.V. Paul.

WEST MEON

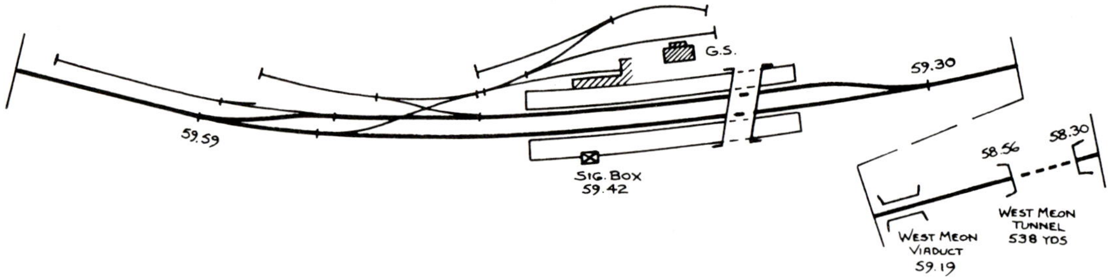

DROXFORD

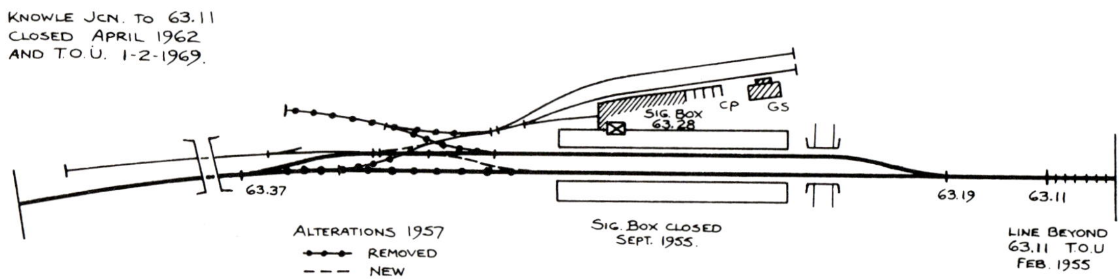

MISLINGFORD GOODS

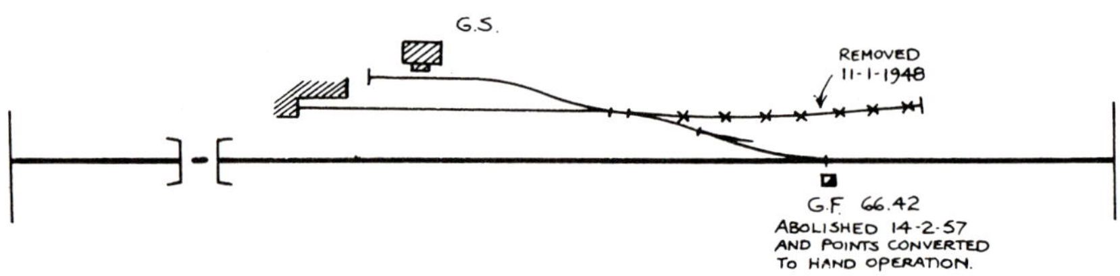

WICKHAM

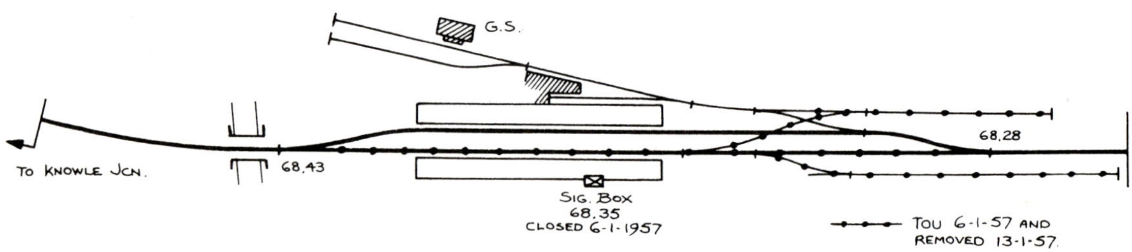

KNOWLE JUNCTION

1907-1921

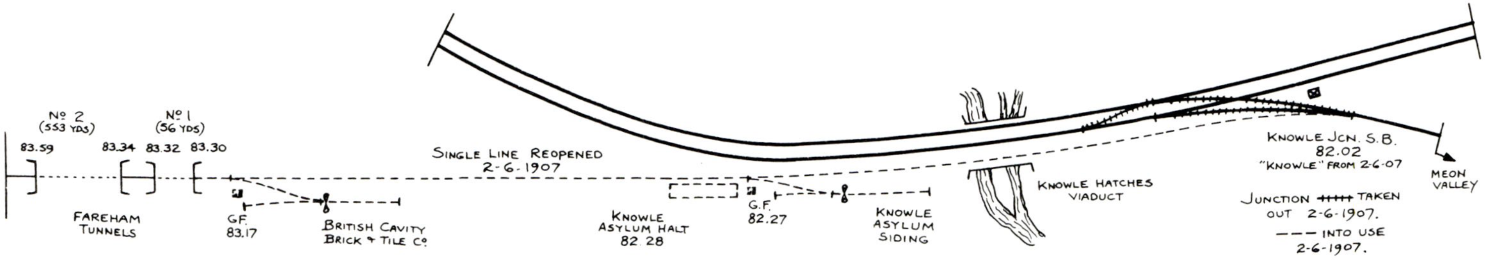

1921-1970

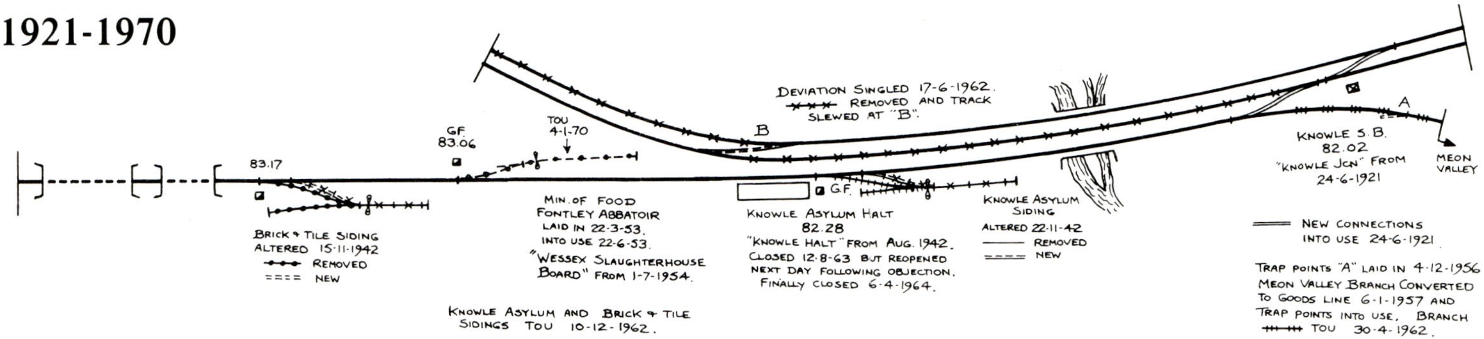

From 1971

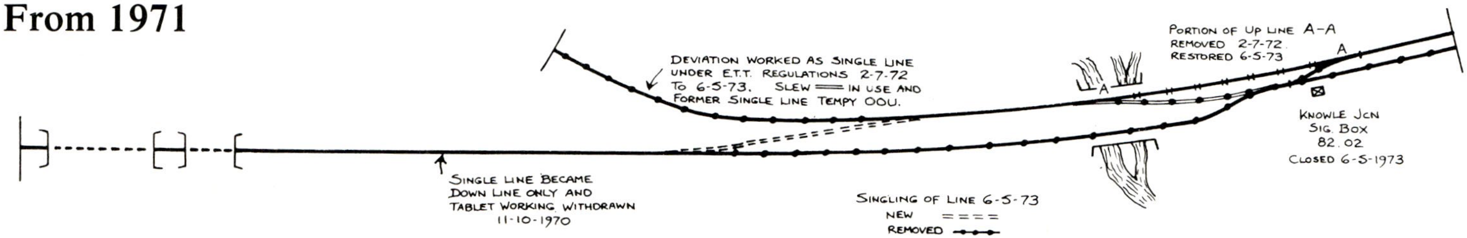

Alton station pictured in the 1980s. Ken Cole.